THE
LEADER YOU ARE

A Journey Through The Emotions
That Shape How You Lead

BLAKE REPINE

Published in Australia in 2025 by Blake Repine

Website: https://www.blakerepine.com.au

© Blake Repine 2025

The moral right of the author has been asserted.

All rights reserved.

Except as permitted under the *Australian Copyright Act 1968* (for example, a fair dealing for the purposes of study, research, criticism, or review), no part of this publication may be reproduced, stored in a retrieval system, communicated or transmitted in any form or by any means without prior written permission.

All enquiries should be directed to the author.

ISBN 9780648841258 (paperback)
ISBN 9780648841265 (ebook)

 A catalogue record for this book is available from the National Library of Australia

Disclaimer

The author has made every effort to ensure the information within this book was correct at the time of publication. The author does not assume and hereby disclaims any liability to any party for any loss, damage, or disruption caused by errors or omissions, whether such errors or omissions result from accident, negligence, or any other cause.

*To all leaders who have ever felt fear, doubt, hope,
or heartache, who have lain awake at night wondering
if they made the right decision, who have carried the burden
quietly, and who have led not just with their minds,
but with their hearts.*

This book is for you.

Acknowledgements

I would like to thank my family for their understanding, support, and love throughout this project. I would also like to thank Luke Richmond for serving as my proofreader and for providing me with encouragement and support.

Contents

Introduction	1
PART ONE – Understanding the Emotional Landscape	3
The Hidden Currents of Leadership	5
Why Emotions Matter	11
The Myth of the Stoic Leader	17
Emotion vs. Emotional Intelligence: Understanding the Difference and Why It Matters	23
The Weight of Responsibility	30
Pressure, Duty, and the Burden of Decision-Making	34
Understanding Emotional Fatigue and Decision Paralysis	40
Personal Reflection: The Cost of Emotional Silence	47
PART TWO – The Leader's Emotional Spectrum	49
Fear and Courage	51
Fear of Failure, Rejection, and Irrelevance	57
Speaking the Truth, Taking Risks, and Being Vulnerable	63
Doubt and Conviction	70
Navigating Impostor Syndrome	76
Building Trust in Your Judgement	82
Joy and Fulfilment	88
The Highs of Achievement and Team Success	94

Finding Meaning in Leadership Beyond Results	100
Anger and Frustration	106
Productive vs. Destructive Anger	112
How to Deal with Injustice, Incompetence, or Betrayal	118
Loneliness and Connection	125
The Isolation of Leadership	131
Building Trusted Relationships and Psychological Safety	137
Hope and Vision	143
The Role of Optimism in Inspiring Others	148
Emotional Energy in Strategic Foresight	154
Personal Reflection: The Emotional Spectrum	160
PART THREE – Emotional Mastery in Action	163
Leading Through Crisis	165
Staying Grounded Under Pressure	171
Pressure as an Opportunity for Influence	175
Regulating Emotion in Turbulent Times	178
Having Difficult Conversations and Conflict	184
Handling Confrontation, Feedback, and Emotionally Charged Moments	190
Balancing Empathy with Accountability	196
The Emotional Culture of a Team	203
How a Leader's Emotions Set the Tone	210
Creating a Resilient, Open, and Safe Team Environment	216
Personal Reflection: The Real Work of Emotional Leadership	223
PART FOUR – Sustaining the Emotional Journey	225
Self-Compassion and Recovery	227
Avoiding Burnout	233
Emotional Self-Care for Sustained Leadership	239

Journalling, Coaching, and Feedback Loops	250
Emotional Growth as a Leadership Edge	256
The Integrated Leader: Wholeness at the Heart of Leadership	263
Leading With Both Head and Heart	269
Embodying Emotional Integrity in Everyday Leadership	275
Personal Reflection: Leadership That Lasts	281
Conclusion: The Journey Home to Self, Team, and Purpose	283
References	289
About the Author	291

Introduction

I've spent most of my adult life learning to lead, first as a soldier, then as an executive and board member, and always, at my core, as a student of people. In various environments, I've made tough calls. Across continents and contexts, one truth has held steady: no matter how strategic, decisive, or disciplined we are, leadership remains deeply and restlessly human.

I still recall a pivotal moment in my career as a civilian leader. After years of leading teams in uniform, where decisiveness and command presence were non-negotiable, I found myself sitting alone in my office, wrestling not with policy but with doubt and loneliness. On paper, the decision before me was clear. Yet beneath the surface, I felt fear. The fear of letting my team down, the fear of being misunderstood, and the fear that perhaps, despite all my training, education, and experience, I no longer had all the answers.

That night, I realised what many leaders eventually discover: strategy and authority will take you far, but what sustains you and earns people's trust is your willingness to feel, to genuinely engage with your emotions, and to guide others through theirs.

The Leader You Are is my attempt to name what often goes unsaid: the hidden currents of emotion that shape how we show up as leaders. This book isn't about presenting a polished image. It's about honouring the reality that leadership can be lonely at times, that doubt and courage coexist, and that our most significant influence comes not from pretending to be invincible but from being genuine.

I've written this book for leaders who feel the weight of responsibility, care deeply about doing right by their teams, and want to lead not just with competence but with heart.

As you read these pages, I invite you to pause, reflect, and be honest with yourself. You don't need to hide the person behind the title. It's your greatest strength.

I hope you enjoy *The Leader You Are*. May it remind you that you're never alone on this journey, and that your emotions are not a weakness but rather the very source of your most significant leadership impact.

PART ONE

Understanding the Emotional Landscape

The Hidden Currents of Leadership

Leadership is often discussed in terms of vision, decision-making, execution, and performance. These visible dimensions are what we measure, plan, and promote. Yet beneath them lie subtler, often unspoken forces, the emotional undercurrents of leadership. Like the unseen currents beneath the ocean's surface, these forces are powerful. They shape how leaders show up, how teams respond, and how organisations succeed or fail.

These hidden emotional dynamics are rarely in the spotlight, yet they are central to influencing, building trust, and fostering sustainable leadership. Understanding them isn't about becoming emotional; it's about becoming emotionally fluent and wise. Leadership, after all, is not simply about directing people; it's about connecting with people. And that connection flows through emotion.

Why Emotions Are the Hidden Currency of Leadership

Emotions are ever-present in leadership, even when they're not discussed. They show up in:

- how a leader enters a room
- the silence between words
- the body language in difficult conversations
- the tension in a team dynamic
- the energy of a disengaged or inspired workforce.

The reality is, people may follow instructions with their minds, but they follow leaders with their hearts. And the heart speaks the language of emotion, trust, fear, inspiration, frustration, care, or anxiety.

Leaders who fail to engage these emotional currents often struggle with blind spots. Their strategies fall flat. Their teams feel unsafe or unseen. Their culture drifts. However, those who learn to feel what lies beneath the surface lead with depth and authenticity.

The Emotional Tone Sets the Cultural Temperature

One of the most powerful yet often overlooked forces in leadership is emotional contagion. A leader's emotional state ripples through their team. Whether they intend to or not, leaders broadcast energy: calm or chaos, confidence or doubt, openness or defensiveness.

This becomes the emotional baseline others adjust to because:
- an anxious leader creates tension
- a leader who is grounded creates stability
- an enthusiastic leader creates momentum
- an emotionally erratic leader creates uncertainty.

Emotions are contagious, and leaders are emotional thermostats. They don't just set direction; they set tone. And tone often determines performance more than policy ever will.

The Unspoken Emotions Behind Leadership Behaviours

Behind every leadership style is an emotional origin story. Consider:
- Micromanagement often masks fear of failure, loss of control, or inadequacy.
- Over-assertiveness may be a shield for insecurity.
- Avoiding confrontation is usually about anxiety or a desire to be liked.
- Perfectionism can stem from shame or self-worth issues.
- Passionate, empowering leadership often flows from hope, purpose, or healed pain.

When leaders explore the emotional roots of their patterns, they don't just change behaviour; they transform their presence.

Navigating the Unseen Emotional Dynamics of a Team

Emotional intelligence isn't just personal; it's collective. Teams operate with emotional histories, unspoken agreements, and group dynamics that shape collaboration and conflict.

A leader tuned into the hidden emotional currents asks:
- What's not being said in this room?
- Where is there trust or a lack of it?
- What emotional risks are people avoiding?
- What tensions are bubbling under the surface?

Reading these signs allows leaders to take action before a breakdown occurs. To surface the unsaid. To tend to the emotional ecosystem that makes high performance possible.

Emotional Suppression vs. Emotional Mastery

Some leaders still believe that emotion has no place in leadership. They suppress it, avoid it, or treat it as a liability. But suppression is not mastery; it is avoidance.

Suppressed emotion doesn't disappear. It leaks out in:
- tone
- passive aggression
- miscommunication
- disengagement
- cultural erosion.

True emotional mastery is not emotional repression; it's emotional integration. Leaders can feel, understand, name, and choose how to act with wisdom and alignment.

This is emotional agility, not reacting impulsively or ignoring emotions but responding intentionally.

Key Hidden Emotional Forces

Fear

Often hidden behind authority or avoidance, fear drives indecision, over-control, or people-pleasing. Naming and confronting it frees up courage.

Shame

This silent force prompts leaders to withdraw, mask their vulnerability, or overcompensate with perfectionism. Shame resilience is key to leading openly and honestly.

Loneliness

Leadership can be isolating. When not acknowledged, this creates disconnection and emotional fatigue. Connection and peer support are critical.

Joy

Often overlooked, joy is a source of creative energy and a key factor in building trust. Celebrating wins and a shared purpose sustains morale and a sense of belonging.

Hope

This quiet strength underlies resilient leadership. Hope helps leaders see through chaos, envision a better future, and inspire action.

Understanding these emotional forces enables leaders to lead with awareness, rather than just reacting.

How to Lead with an Awareness of Emotional Undercurrents

Pause and Feel

Start meetings with an emotional check-in. Pause during the day and ask yourself, "What's happening emotionally in me and around me?"

Reflect on Patterns

After difficult conversations, ask, "What was I feeling? What did the other person feel? What went unspoken?"

Create Emotional Safety

Encourage truth-telling, vulnerability, and emotional expression without punishment. Model it yourself.

Use Emotionally Intelligent Language

Instead of "What's the problem?" ask, "What are you feeling about this situation?"

Instead of "Just stick to the facts," ask, "What's the emotional temperature here?"

Work With a Coach or Reflective Partner

Sometimes, you need an external mirror to help uncover what you can't see on your own. Emotional blind spots are best explored with the support of a trusted individual.

When Leaders Embrace Emotional Depth

When leaders embrace the emotional side of leadership:
- People feel more connected and committed.
- Culture becomes more resilient and open.
- Conflict becomes productive instead of corrosive.
- Strategy becomes energised by meaning.
- The organisation becomes more human.

This doesn't require therapy in the boardroom. It involves empathy in the leadership room. Emotional insight. Curiosity. Presence. The courage to name what is often left unspoken.

Lead Beneath the Surface

Leadership isn't just about what's above the surface: goals, charts, and directives. It's about what flows beneath: emotions, beliefs, tensions, and trust.

The best leaders are not just masters of execution. They are stewards of emotional reality. They can walk into a room, sense the atmosphere, and respond with authenticity and groundedness.

The hidden currents are always there. You can ignore them. Or you can learn to read them and lead through them.

That's where leadership becomes transformational. That's where leaders stop managing outcomes and start shaping meaningful influence.

And that's where your deepest leadership potential lies, not above the surface but below it.

Why Emotions Matter

Leadership is often perceived as a realm governed by logic, strategy, and decision-making prowess. While these attributes are vital, they only paint part of the picture. The reality is that leadership is deeply human, and at the core of human experience lies emotion. Emotions shape our perceptions, guide our behaviours, and influence the quality of our relationships. For leaders, understanding, managing, and leveraging emotions, both their own and those of others, is not optional. It is fundamental to effective leadership.

The Emotional Foundation of Leadership

At its core, leadership is about people. Whether it's inspiring a team, managing conflict, navigating change, or building a culture, leaders are constantly influencing and being influenced by those around them. Emotions are the invisible currents beneath these interactions. A leader's ability to connect, empathise, and motivate relies heavily on emotional intelligence, a concept made popular by psychologist Daniel Goleman[1]. Emotional intelligence includes self-awareness,

---

1. (Goleman, *Emotional Intelligence: Why it can matter more than IQ*, 2020)

self-regulation, motivation, empathy, and social skills. These elements enable leaders to be both practical and human.

High emotional intelligence enables leaders to remain composed under pressure, deliver difficult feedback with compassion, and make values-driven decisions, even in the face of uncertainty. Conversely, leaders who ignore or mishandle emotions often struggle with engagement, team dynamics, and trust.

Emotions Drive Decision-Making

While we often like to believe our decisions are rational, neuroscience reveals a different perspective. Emotions play a critical role in how we process information and make decisions. The limbic system, which governs our emotional responses, is intricately linked with our cognitive processes. When leaders are emotionally aware, they're better able to balance instinct with intellect, ensuring that decisions are not only efficient but also ethical and sustainable.

Moreover, emotions help signal what matters most. A sense of urgency, concern, or excitement often draws attention to issues that require attention. Leaders who are attuned to these emotional cues, both within themselves and their teams, can respond more thoughtfully and proactively. Ignoring emotional signals can lead to misjudging situations, delaying necessary action, or making tone-deaf choices that alienate others.

The Role of Self-Awareness

Self-awareness is the cornerstone of emotional intelligence. Leaders who understand their emotional patterns can better manage their reactions and behaviours. For example, recognising a tendency to become defensive in high-stakes meetings allows a leader to pause, reflect, and choose a more constructive response. This not only improves personal performance but also models emotional maturity for the team.

Without self-awareness, emotions can hijack decision-making, damage relationships, and undermine credibility. A leader who frequently lashes out under stress or disengages when faced with criticism sends the message that emotions are to be feared or suppressed. This creates a culture of avoidance and distrust. On the other hand, emotionally aware leaders foster psychological safety, encouraging openness, innovation, and resilience.

Empathy and Connection

Empathy, the ability to understand and share the emotions of others, is a powerful tool in leadership. It's what enables leaders to see beyond the surface and connect with what truly motivates their team members. Empathetic leaders listen actively, recognise non-verbal cues, and validate others' experiences. This doesn't mean agreeing with everyone or avoiding difficult conversations. It means showing that people matter and that their perspectives are valued.

Empathy strengthens trust, which is the foundation of any high-performing team. When people feel seen and heard, they are more likely to be engaged, loyal, and committed to their work. In contrast, leaders who dismiss or overlook emotional needs risk fostering disengagement and turnover. Particularly in times of change or crisis, empathy becomes a stabilising force. A leader who acknowledges the emotional impact of a restructuring, for instance, helps people process uncertainty and move forward with greater clarity.

Culture and Emotional Contagion

Emotions are contagious. A leader's emotional state can ripple through an organisation, influencing morale, energy, and performance. Leaders who consistently exhibit optimism, gratitude, and calm are likely to see those traits reflected in them. Conversely, chronic negativity, anxiety, or aloofness can demoralise teams and undermine culture.

This emotional contagion makes emotional discipline a key aspect of leadership. It's not about being inauthentic or hiding emotions, but about being intentional. Leaders set the emotional tone. They must learn to regulate their emotional expressions in ways that are both genuine and constructive. Celebrating wins, acknowledging losses, and remaining present in tense moments sends a powerful message: emotions matter here, and they're handled with care.

Leading Through Change and Adversity

Emotions often run high during periods of change, conflict, or uncertainty. These moments test a leader's emotional capacity and resilience. Effective leaders don't pretend emotions don't exist; they embrace them. They address fears, manage resistance, and help their teams find meaning in new realities. They acknowledge the grief that often accompanies change while also inspiring hope and a vision for the future.

This emotional navigation develops credibility and unity. People are more inclined to follow a leader who can create space for discomfort while mapping out a clear, compassionate path ahead. In tough times, emotional presence is not a luxury; it's a lifeline.

Emotions and Ethical Leadership

Emotions also play a central role in moral reasoning. Compassion, guilt, pride, and outrage help guide ethical behaviour. A leader who feels deeply about fairness, for example, is more likely to challenge inequities and advocate for integrity. Emotional sensitivity to harm, justice, and human dignity helps leaders stay anchored in values, even when it's inconvenient or unpopular.

Ethical lapses in leadership are often linked to emotional disconnection, where ambition, pressure, or apathy take precedence over empathy and conscience. Leaders who stay emotionally engaged are less likely to make decisions that harm people or compromise their values for short-term gain.

Developing Emotional Literacy

Given the importance of emotions in leadership, developing emotional literacy is essential. Leaders must build their ability to identify, articulate, and regulate emotions in themselves and others. This begins with self-reflection and receiving feedback. Leadership development programs should incorporate training in emotional intelligence, coaching, and experiential learning to enhance overall effectiveness.

Simple practices such as journalling, mindfulness, or asking, "How am I feeling right now?" can cultivate emotional awareness. Building habits of gratitude, perspective-taking, and vulnerability also enhances emotional effectiveness. Importantly, leaders should create environments where emotions can be discussed openly and constructively, removing the stigma often associated with emotional expression.

Human First, Leader Always

In a world of increasing complexity and technological disruption, the human aspect of leadership is more vital than ever. Emotions are not distractions from leadership; they are central to it. Leaders who grasp and utilise emotions are better positioned to cultivate trust, encourage engagement, and achieve meaningful results. They lead not only with their minds but with their hearts.

As we look to the future, the most effective leaders will not be those who suppress their emotions, but those who acknowledge and embrace them. They will be emotionally intelligent, empathetic, and authentic. They will recognise that leadership is not just about strategy and execution; it is about relationships, meaning, and care.

Ultimately, people don't just follow titles; they follow leaders who make them feel safe, valued, and inspired. That is the power of emotions in leadership and why they matter more than ever.

The Myth of the Stoic Leader

For centuries, the idea of the "stoic leader" has been revered in boardrooms, battlefields, and bureaucracies. This archetype, the calm, unemotional, rock-solid figure who never flinches, complains, or reveals vulnerability, has been held up as the gold standard of leadership. In many ways, it is rooted in the ancient philosophy of Stoicism, which emphasises the importance of reason, self-control, and emotional mastery. However, over time, this concept has become distorted. What was initially intended to cultivate inner strength has become, in many contexts, a mask for emotional repression and disconnection.

The modern myth of the stoic leader suggests that strong leaders must be emotionally detached, unshakably composed, and resistant to vulnerability. In reality, this myth often undermines the very effectiveness it seeks to uphold. Today's most impactful leaders are not those who hide their emotions but those who understand, embrace, and skilfully express them. Emotional intelligence, authenticity, and human connection are now critical components of effective leadership. It's time to challenge and deconstruct the myth of the stoic leader.

Origins of the Stoic Ideal

Stoicism, a philosophy developed by thinkers such as Epictetus, Seneca, and Marcus Aurelius, promotes rational thinking, self-awareness, and resilience in the face of adversity. At its core, it teaches that we cannot control external events; only our responses to them can be controlled. These concepts are highly relevant for leadership, especially during times of crisis or change. However, ancient Stoicism was never about suppressing emotions. Instead, it focused on emotional mastery, recognising emotions, understanding their origins, and responding wisely.

Unfortunately, the term "stoic" has been co-opted and simplified into a cultural shorthand for emotional distance. The stoic leader, in popular imagination, is one who never shows fear, doubt, or sadness. They soldier on, unaffected by criticism or conflict. However, this version of stoicism often leads to leaders who are isolated, emotionally unavailable, and disconnected from the people they serve.

The Problem with Emotional Repression

The myth of the stoic leader creates unrealistic expectations. It teaches leaders, either implicitly or explicitly, that emotions are a liability. This mindset can be particularly pervasive in traditionally masculine or high-pressure leadership environments, such as the military, politics, or corporate finance. Leaders in these fields may be praised for "keeping it together" while quietly suffering under the burden of stress, anxiety, or loneliness.

This suppression of emotion doesn't make leaders stronger; it makes them brittle. Bottled-up feelings don't disappear; they fester. Repressed emotion can lead to burnout, mental health issues, poor communication, and relational breakdowns. Moreover, it sets a dangerous precedent for organisational culture. If leaders model emotional detachment, team members may feel discouraged from voicing concerns, expressing vulnerability, or seeking support.

In contrast, leaders who acknowledge and appropriately share their emotional experiences create psychologically safe environments. These spaces foster trust, innovation, and resilience. Vulnerability does not weaken a leader's authority; it humanises it.

The Power of Emotional Intelligence

One of the most significant leadership insights of the past two decades is the importance of emotional intelligence. Leaders with high emotional intelligence are self-aware, empathetic, and capable of managing both their own emotions and the emotional dynamics of their teams. They are more effective at building relationships, resolving conflict, and motivating others.

Ironically, many of the outcomes sought by the myth of the stoic leader—calm under pressure, rational decision-making, and strength in adversity—are more reliably achieved through emotional intelligence than through suppression. A leader who engages in self-reflection and understands their emotional triggers and values is far more effective than one who represses everything.

Authentic stoicism, when understood correctly, can align with emotional intelligence. It involves not being ruled by emotions, but it does not mean pretending they don't exist. It means remaining centred while still fully engaging with the human experience.

Vulnerability Builds Trust

Perhaps the most destructive aspect of the stoic leader myth is the belief that vulnerability equates to weakness. Vulnerability is one of the most powerful tools in a leader's arsenal. When leaders admit they don't have all the answers, apologise when they're wrong, or share their struggles, they invite connection. This transparency builds trust and fosters loyalty.

Brené Brown, a prominent researcher on vulnerability and leadership, asserts that "vulnerability is the birthplace of courage, creativity, and innovation."[2] It enables teams to take risks, learn from failure, and engage authentically. Leaders who embrace vulnerability foster cultures where others feel safe to do the same.

Of course, vulnerability should be balanced with discernment. Oversharing or emotional dumping can be inappropriate. However, when practised with emotional intelligence, vulnerability becomes a sign of strength, not fragility.

The Stoic Mask and Its Costs

Leaders who buy into the stoic myth often end up wearing a mask. They present a version of themselves that is always in control, always confident, and always composed. Over time, this performance can lead to identity dissonance, a gap between the leader's actual identity and how they perceive themselves. This disconnect can erode personal wellbeing, reduce authenticity, and create a sense of isolation.

It also makes it harder for team members to connect with them. People don't relate to perfection; they relate to humanity. A leader who never expresses emotion can become unapproachable and even intimidating. Their team may

---

2. (Brown, 2010)

hesitate to speak honestly, raise concerns, or share feedback. Innovation suffers. Engagement declines.

The cost isn't just personal; it's organisational. Cultures shaped by stoic leadership often discourage emotional expression, leading to poor morale, weak collaboration, and a limited diversity of thought. In contrast, emotionally open leaders nurture cultures of empathy, inclusion, and high performance.

Embracing a New Leadership Narrative

The future of leadership isn't about stoic detachment; it's about emotional integration. Leaders need to move beyond the binary of "tough or tender" and "rational or emotional." They must be both principled and present, decisive and compassionate, resilient and genuine.

This doesn't mean abandoning self-discipline or courage. It means expanding the definition of strength to include emotional honesty. It means recognising that emotional presence, far from being a liability, is a strategic advantage.

As generational expectations change and workforces become more diverse, emotionally intelligent leadership is no longer optional; it is expected. Younger employees, in particular, value leaders who are empathetic, authentic, and emotionally available. They want to work in environments where they can bring their whole selves to work. Leaders who cling to outdated stoic ideals risk becoming irrelevant or ineffective.

Redefining Strength in Leadership

The myth of the stoic leader served a purpose in a different time. It helped navigate war, hardship, and industrial-era leadership models that prioritised hierarchy over humanity.

However, the world has changed, and our models of leadership must change as well.

Real strength lies not in suppressing emotion but in understanding it; not in projecting invulnerability but in building genuine connections. Today's most effective leaders are those who lead with both heart and mind, embracing complexity, expressing compassion, and modelling emotional maturity.

It's time to retire the myth of the stoic leader and replace it with something more powerful: the emotionally intelligent, self-aware, courageous human leader. Not only does this approach create better outcomes, it also reflects the truth of what leadership is: a profoundly human endeavour.

Emotion vs. Emotional Intelligence: Understanding the Difference and Why It Matters

In the realm of leadership, relationships, and personal development, two terms frequently appear: emotion and emotional intelligence. While often used interchangeably, they refer to fundamentally different concepts. Emotion is instinctive and universal, something all humans experience. Emotional intelligence, on the other hand, is a skill set, a learned ability to recognise, understand, manage, and influence emotions in ourselves and others.

Understanding the difference between emotion and emotional intelligence is crucial not only for personal growth but also for developing stronger teams, making better decisions, and leading effectively. Emotions are inevitable, while emotional intelligence dictates how we respond to them.

What Are Emotions?

Emotions are complex psychological states comprising three key components: a subjective experience (our internal emotional experience), a physiological response (like changes in heart rate or hormone levels), and a behavioural or expressive response (such as facial expressions or actions).

Emotions are automatic and instinctive. They have evolved as survival mechanisms to help humans react to their environment. Fear triggers the fight-or-flight response. Anger prepares us for confrontation, while joy fosters social bonding. Sadness may signify a need for support. Whether we realise it or not, emotions are always present and influencing our thoughts and behaviours.

Importantly, emotions are neither good nor bad; they are neutral indicators of how we process our experiences. However, our responses to them can lead to positive or negative consequences.

What Is Emotional Intelligence?

Let's dig deeper into emotional intelligence. Emotional intelligence encompasses the ability to perceive, understand, manage, and utilise emotions effectively. While emotions are reactive and spontaneous, emotional intelligence is reflective and strategic. Emotional Intelligence is not about suppressing emotions but rather about handling them constructively in a way that aligns with one's values and goals.

Goleman[3] outlines five key components of emotional intelligence:

1. **Self-awareness:** the ability to recognise and understand your own emotions and how they affect your thoughts and behaviour.
2. **Self-regulation:** the ability to manage or redirect your emotional impulses and respond appropriately.

---

3. (Goleman, *Working with emotional intelligence*, 1998)

3. *Motivation*: the drive to pursue goals with energy and persistence, often influenced by emotional resilience and optimism.
4. *Empathy*: the capacity to understand the emotions of others and consider their perspectives.
5. **Social skills**: the ability to manage relationships, influence others, communicate effectively, and work well in teams.

Together, these skills enable individuals to navigate interpersonal relationships with greater judgement and empathy, making emotional intelligence a vital factor in achieving personal and professional success.

Emotion vs. Emotional Intelligence: Key Differences

Aspect	Emotion	Emotional Intelligence
Definition	A natural, instinctive state of mind resulting from circumstances or relationships	The ability to identify, manage, and influence emotions in oneself and others
Origin	Innate, automatic response rooted in biology	Learned and developed over time through self-awareness and practice
Control	Largely unconscious and involuntary	Conscious, intentional, and adaptive
Function	Alerts us to what's essential; drives action	Helps us manage our response to emotions and build effective relationships
Outcome	Can lead to reactive, impulsive behaviour if unmanaged	Supports thoughtful, value-aligned behaviour and decisions

In essence, emotion is what you feel; emotional intelligence is how you respond to it.

Why Emotional Intelligence Matters

Improved Decision-Making

Every decision we make is emotionally charged. Without emotional intelligence, leaders may overreact, misjudge a situation, or overlook the emotional consequences of their actions. A person high in emotional intelligence is better equipped to pause, reflect, and choose a balanced response. They weigh emotional input alongside logic, resulting in more ethical, measured, and thoughtful decisions.

Better Relationships

Strong relationships are built on mutual understanding, respect, and effective communication, all of which are rooted in emotional intelligence. Those who lack EI often struggle with empathy, misread emotional cues, or react defensively. In contrast, emotionally intelligent individuals listen actively, respond with care, and navigate conflict with grace.

Enhanced Leadership

Leadership is about influence, and influence requires an emotional connection. Emotionally intelligent leaders are attuned to the emotional landscape of their teams. They recognise when morale is low, when conflict is simmering, or when recognition is needed. By managing their own emotions and responding skilfully to others, they build trust, loyalty, and engagement.

Greater Resilience

EI helps people manage stress, bounce back from setbacks, and keep their perspective. While emotions such as fear, anger, or sadness are unavoidable, those with emotional intelligence can process these feelings constructively. They are less likely to be overwhelmed by their emotions and are better equipped to remain grounded in challenging situations.

Can Emotional Intelligence Be Developed?

Absolutely. Unlike IQ, which tends to remain relatively stable, emotional intelligence can be developed at any stage of life. Enhancing emotional intelligence starts with increasing self-awareness, recognising emotional triggers, accurately naming emotions, and understanding how they influence behaviour.

From there, individuals can work on:
- mindfulness practices to enhance emotional regulation
- journalling or reflection to understand emotional patterns
- active listening to improve empathy
- feedback from trusted peers or mentors to gain insight into social behaviours.

Organisations can also foster EI development through coaching, training programs, and emotionally intelligent leadership models.

Common Misconceptions

Emotional Intelligence Means Being "Nice" All the Time

Emotional intelligence doesn't mean avoiding tough conversations or being too agreeable. Emotionally intelligent individuals often excel at delivering hard truths with respect and clarity. They are assertive, not passive.

High EI Means Suppressing Emotions

Suppressing emotion isn't emotional intelligence; it's avoidance. Actual EI involves acknowledging emotions, understanding them, and choosing the best way to express or act on them.

Emotions Should Be Removed from Decision-Making

Removing emotion from decisions is both impossible and unwise. Emotions provide valuable insights into our needs, values, and instincts. Emotional intelligence enables us to utilise emotions to make more informed decisions, rather than ignoring them.

Real-World Example: A Tale of Two Leaders

Imagine two executives facing an unexpected crisis. The first becomes visibly frustrated, dismisses their team's concerns, and rushes into action without considering the emotional impact on their team. The second takes a moment to acknowledge their stress, gathers the team, listens to their concerns, and communicates with empathy and clarity.

Both experience the same emotions, but only the second demonstrates emotional intelligence. The outcome is not just a more effective response; it's a stronger, more united team.

Integrating Emotion and Emotional Intelligence

Emotions are part of what makes us human. They inform, energise, and guide us. However, when left unchecked, they can lead to reactivity and regret. Emotional intelligence enables us to harness the power of emotion constructively.

The goal is not to eliminate emotion but to integrate it, honouring its role while remaining self-aware and intentional. As we navigate increasingly complex personal and professional landscapes, emotional intelligence is no longer a "nice-to-have". It is a fundamental capability.

By grasping the distinction between emotion and emotional intelligence, we unlock the capacity to lead with empathy, communicate effectively, and live with a greater sense of purpose.

The Weight of Responsibility

Leadership is often celebrated for its perks, authority, influence, and recognition. Yet beneath these visible rewards lies a profound and frequently invisible truth: leadership carries weight. This weight is the responsibility that comes with being accountable not only for results but also for people, values, and the long-term health of an organisation or community. To lead is to shoulder the burdens of others, make decisions that affect lives, and be the moral and strategic compass in times of uncertainty. That is no light load.

The Nature of Responsibility

At its core, responsibility in leadership isn't just about fulfilling duties; it's about ownership. Leaders are accountable for setting vision and direction; they are also answerable for outcomes, both good and bad. They must navigate competing interests, conflicting values, and imperfect information. When things go wrong, they should be the ones who step forward, not back.

Authentic leadership means being responsible for more than just yourself. It involves shouldering the hopes, fears, and wellbeing of others. When an organisation faces hardship or a team struggles, leaders are expected to absorb the shock and forge a path forward. This demand for emotional resilience and strategic clarity is relentless.

Responsibility for People

One of the most profound aspects of leadership responsibility is the duty of care towards others. Every decision, from restructuring a team to cutting a budget, carries human implications. Leaders are accountable for creating an environment where people feel valued, safe, and empowered. When that environment is compromised, the responsibility for correction and accountability falls directly on leadership.

Leaders must also create space for others' emotional experiences. They are expected to lead with compassion while striking a balance between performance and productivity. This emotional labour is often unrecognised but is a central part of the burden leaders bear.

Responsibility for Culture and Ethics

Leadership responsibility encompasses upholding values and maintaining a strong culture. Whether formally stated or informally modelled, leaders influence the ethical climate of their organisations. When a leader disregards misconduct or tolerates toxic behaviour, it signals that such behaviours are acceptable. This leads to long-term cultural decay.

On the other hand, responsible leaders establish a culture of integrity, transparency, and accountability. They recognise that trust is delicate and that a leader's actions must match their words. Meeting this standard, particularly under pressure, is both a privilege and a significant burden.

Being the Final Decision-Maker

Another aspect of leadership weight is the loneliness that comes with ultimate accountability. While inclusive leadership is essential, there are times when decisions must be made alone. Leaders are the ones who must say yes or no when there is no consensus. They must choose between competing priorities and bear the consequences, even when outcomes are uncertain.

This "burden of finality" creates stress and emotional fatigue. Making high-stakes decisions that impact people's livelihoods, reputations, or futures is a challenging task. Leaders must learn to navigate ambiguity, risk, and the moral complexity of never having perfect answers.

The Invisible Toll

The weight of responsibility often manifests in unseen ways, such as sleepless nights, emotional exhaustion, anxiety, or self-doubt. Leaders maintain a mental and emotional ledger of unfinished tasks, unresolved conflicts, and unmet expectations. And because leadership often demands composure, many internalise these burdens instead of expressing them.

Without proper support or self-awareness, this hidden toll can lead to burnout, poor decision-making, or disconnection from others. That's why responsible leadership must include self-responsibility for physical health, mental well-being, and sustainable pacing.

Delegation Without Abdication

One of the ways responsible leaders manage their weight is by empowering others. Delegation isn't about offloading responsibility; it's about building capability and trust. Nonetheless, the leader remains ultimately accountable.

Effective delegation requires emotional maturity, which involves letting go of control while maintaining oversight.

Leaders who hoard responsibility stifle growth, while those who abdicate it create chaos. Responsible leadership means knowing what to hold tightly, what to release, and when to do each.

Role Modelling Responsibility

Perhaps the most profound impact of leadership responsibility is its modelling. When leaders admit mistakes, take accountability, and remain calm under pressure, they teach others what responsibility looks like. They cultivate cultures where people feel safe taking ownership of their actions and learning from them.

Conversely, leaders who deflect blame or shy away from hard truths undermine trust. Their teams learn to look after themselves instead of stepping up to the plate. Responsibility is contagious, for both its presence and its absence.

The Quiet Weight; The Noble Duty

The weight of leadership isn't always visible. It's often found in the pause before a difficult conversation, the late-night review of a struggling project, or the quiet reflection that follows a tough decision. It's felt in moments of doubt, grief, or guilt when the outcomes don't meet expectations. Yet it's also what makes leadership meaningful.

True leaders don't seek to escape this weight; they aim to carry it well. They cultivate the resilience to endure it, the wisdom to navigate it, and the humility to share it when necessary. Leadership isn't a crown; it's a load borne with grace. By holding it well, leaders earn something far greater than authority: trust, respect, and the right to lead others forward.

Pressure, Duty, and the Burden of Decision-Making

Leadership is synonymous with decision-making. Every day, leaders are called upon to make judgements, some minor and others with profound implications. With these decisions comes an immense sense of duty and often pressure that few outside the role can fully comprehend. A leader does not merely choose between options; they carry the weight of implications, people's expectations, reputational risks, and long-term consequences. This complex interplay between duty and pressure shapes the emotional landscape of leadership, defining its moral and strategic challenges.

The Nature of Leadership Pressure

Pressure in leadership arises from the convergence of responsibility, visibility, and consequence. Every decision a leader makes is scrutinised, not just for its outcome but also for how it aligns with values, principles, and stakeholders' expectations. Whether it's an operational call in a crisis or a strategic shift in direction, the pressure to "get it right" is constant and inescapable.

Time constraints, imperfect information, and competing priorities intensify this pressure. The real world seldom presents problems with clear-cut answers. Leaders frequently navigate grey areas, where every option involves trade-offs and no choice is without cost. What heightens the pressure is the knowledge that others—employees, partners, and communities—are affected by the outcome.

Duty as a Leadership Compass

In the face of relentless pressure, duty becomes the leader's internal compass. It is a moral and professional obligation to act in service of others and in support of the mission at hand. Duty anchors a leader when clarity is elusive. It reminds them that leadership is not about comfort or convenience but about stewardship and sacrifice.

Leaders with a profound sense of duty do not pursue popularity or convenience. Integrity, ethics, and a commitment to service guide their actions. This often means making the more difficult choice, the less popular decision, or opting for the course of action that may cause short-term pain but benefits the organisation or community in the long run.

Duty also encompasses accountability. A leader takes responsibility for the outcomes of their decisions, even when those results attract criticism or lead to failure. The burden of duty can be substantial, but it is what distinguishes authentic leadership from mere management or authority.

The Decision-Making Burden

Unlike many roles where decisions are made collaboratively or escalated upwards, leadership often falls solely on you. The buck stops with the leader. This can be a lonely experience, especially when decisions carry high stakes and are emotionally charged.

For example, consider a CEO faced with the decision to implement layoffs to keep a business afloat. There are no good choices, only necessary ones. The burden lies not just in making the decision but in delivering it with empathy, preparing for the aftermath, and enduring the long-term emotional consequences.

Another challenge is that many leadership decisions must be made with incomplete information. There's no time to wait for all the facts. Leaders must decide with what they have and stand by those decisions. This is the essence of the burden: acting with imperfect knowledge and living with the consequences.

Conflicting Stakeholder Expectations

A significant source of decision-making pressure arises from stakeholders, boards, staff, customers, community members, and regulators, each with distinct, sometimes conflicting expectations. Leaders must navigate these pressures without alienating key relationships or compromising their integrity.

Balancing these perspectives requires discernment and emotional strength. Leaders often face criticism, regardless of the choices they make. Realising that your decision might upset or deeply disappoint people can create emotional strain. The burden lies not only in making choices but also in owning their consequences.

Emotional Cost of Leadership Decisions

Over time, this pressure and duty can take a toll. The emotional cost of decision-making isn't always visible, but it is genuine. Leaders may internalise the fallout from tough calls, second-guess themselves, ruminate, or feel guilty. Some individuals experience compassion fatigue, particularly in roles that involve people, such as healthcare or local government. Others suffer from decision fatigue, a mental exhaustion caused by the constant need to evaluate, choose, and reassess.

This cost is amplified when decisions lead to unintended consequences. A well-intentioned change might result in unforeseen harm. The leader carries that burden, often in silence. Without support outlets, this can contribute to burnout, withdrawal, or cynicism.

Strategies for Managing the Burden

Clarify Values and Priorities

In moments of uncertainty, values serve as the best guide. Leaders who have clearly defined their principles, such as transparency, fairness, or long-term stewardship, can navigate tough decisions with more confidence. Values act as filters, narrowing choices and aligning actions with a greater purpose.

Build Decision-Making Frameworks

Effective leaders develop decision-making frameworks that involve assessing impact, consulting stakeholders, considering long-term implications, and testing for bias. While these frameworks don't eliminate pressure, they provide structure and help to reduce impulsivity.

Lean on Trusted Advisors

Leaders shouldn't make decisions in isolation. Having a circle of trusted confidants or mentors, people who provide honest input without any agenda, helps lighten the emotional and intellectual load. It also guards against blind spots.

Practice Emotional Regulation

Pressure is inevitable, but how leaders respond to it can be managed. Practices such as mindfulness, journalling, or reflective walks help process stress and maintain emotional clarity. Leaders who invest in emotional regulation are less reactive and more composed.

Communicate the "Why"

When decisions are tough, clear communication is essential. Explaining the rationale behind a decision, even when people disagree, shows transparency and respect. This can help mitigate backlash and encourage a better understanding.

Leadership Under Prolonged Pressure

Some leaders function under constant, unrelenting pressure, whether from crises, politics, or organisational dysfunction. In these situations, the burden can become corrosive. Leaders may begin to suppress emotions, withdraw from engagement, or lose their sense of purpose.

In these moments, reconnecting with the "why"—why you lead, why the work matters, and why the mission endures—can restore strength. It's also crucial to seek support. Leadership may be lonely, but it doesn't have to be solitary.

Mental health care, peer networks, and executive coaching are essential tools for managing the psychological burden of decision-making. Requesting help is not a sign of weakness; rather, it is a hallmark of self-aware and sustainable leadership.

Strength Through Stewardship

Pressure, duty, and decision-making aren't obstacles to leadership; they're vital elements of it. The readiness to step forward when others hold back, to make tough decisions in service of others, and to bear the burden without losing your humanity—this is what truly defines leadership.

The burden is real, but it is also noble. It calls forth the best in those who respond to it with courage, humility, and care. Leaders who recognise this burden and learn to carry it with wisdom are the ones who endure, not just in their roles but in the legacy they leave behind.

Understanding Emotional Fatigue and Decision Paralysis

Emotional fatigue and decision paralysis are two interconnected psychological challenges that significantly impact leaders under prolonged stress. They represent the cumulative toll of sustained emotional labour, constant decision-making, and the ongoing need to maintain composure and clarity in the face of complexity. When left unaddressed, these conditions can erode effectiveness, wellbeing, and morale, both personally and organisationally.

What Is Emotional Fatigue?

Emotional fatigue, often referred to as emotional exhaustion, is the sensation of being emotionally overextended and drained. It usually arises from chronic stress, significant empathy demands, and the ongoing regulation of one's own emotions. For leaders, this is particularly prevalent in high-stakes or people-centric roles, where they must often absorb the feelings of others while downplaying or sidelining their own.

Symptoms may include:

- feeling numb or detached from work and people
- difficulty concentrating or engaging with tasks
- increased irritability, anxiety, or cynicism
- loss of motivation or sense of meaning.

Emotional fatigue is not a sign of weakness; rather, it indicates emotional overload. Leaders frequently suppress these symptoms to uphold the façade of strength, which only intensifies the fatigue.

Sources of Emotional Fatigue in Leadership

Emotional Containment

Leaders are expected to manage their emotions in public, remain calm during crises, be confident in the face of uncertainty, and remain composed when facing criticism. While this emotional restraint can sometimes be necessary, it can also become exhausting over time.

Constant Support of Others

Leaders often serve as the emotional anchor for their teams. They absorb the stress, fears, and frustrations of others while managing their own. Over time, this can lead to compassion fatigue, a distinct form of emotional exhaustion that impacts those who regularly provide care or engage in emotional labour.

Role Complexity and Ambiguity

When a leader's responsibilities are extensive and constantly changing, it can lead to decision fatigue, value conflicts, and identity strain, all of which contribute to emotional exhaustion.

Moral Injury and Ethical Strain

Making decisions that conflict with personal values or harm others, regardless of necessity, can lead to moral distress, another contributor to emotional fatigue.

What Is Decision Paralysis?

Decision paralysis refers to the inability to make or act on a decision, often stemming from the fear of making the wrong choice. It can be situational, impacting one significant decision, or chronic, evolving into a recurring pattern. For leaders, decision paralysis poses particular risks, as it slows momentum, erodes confidence, and undermines the trust others place in them.

It is often caused by:

- **overwhelm** from too many options or too much information
- **fear of failure**, particularly in visible or high-risk scenarios
- **perfectionism**, leading to the desire to find the "perfect" decision
- **low energy or burnout**, reducing cognitive capacity for processing.

Decision paralysis is not just a matter of indecision; it indicates that cognitive and emotional resources have been overtaxed.

The Link Between Emotional Fatigue and Decision Paralysis

The two phenomena often reinforce each other. Emotional fatigue can impair mental clarity, leading to slower thinking and a lower risk tolerance. The mental and emotional effort required to make decisions becomes increasingly complex, leading leaders to begin delaying, deferring, or altogether avoiding making decisions.

This avoidance breeds anxiety, as unresolved issues accumulate. The longer a decision is delayed, the heavier it becomes, creating a self-reinforcing loop. The leader may begin to question their competence, which can fuel imposter syndrome and worsen emotional depletion.

Consequences for Individuals and Organisations

Unchecked emotional fatigue and decision paralysis can lead to:

- *Erosion of credibility*: Delayed decisions and inconsistent leadership undermine trust within teams and among stakeholders.
- *Loss of morale*: Teams can sense when a leader is disengaged or immobilised. This often leads to confusion, frustration, and a drop in motivation.
- *Decreased performance*: Emotional exhaustion and cognitive overload impede problem-solving ability and innovation.
- *Physical health decline*: Chronic stress leads to various health problems, such as insomnia, headaches, digestive issues, and cardiovascular concerns.

For the organisation, these conditions can hinder progress, elevate turnover, and diminish resilience during periods of change or crisis.

Strategies for Managing Emotional Fatigue

Emotional Boundaries

Create a space between your role and your identity. While being emotionally present is vital, absorbing every emotional wave in the organisation is unsustainable. Learn to support others without internalising every problem.

Schedule Recovery

Leadership recovery is not passive. Allocate time for mental stillness, meaningful connection, and physical rest, without guilt. Recovery should be intentional and regular.

Reflection and Processing

Engage in journalling, coaching, or peer debriefing to process tough decisions and emotions. Don't carry them alone. Processing lightens the invisible mental load and creates space for renewal.

Name the Weight

Allow yourself and others to recognise and name emotional fatigue when it arises. Naming fosters a shared understanding and can help reduce feelings of isolation; leaders who acknowledge their struggles demonstrate emotional intelligence and strength.

Strategies for Preventing Decision Paralysis

Establish Decision Frameworks

Utilise predefined frameworks (e.g., cost-benefit analysis, Eisenhower Matrix, SWOT) to make complex decisions simpler. This shifts the focus from personal perfection to structured evaluation.

Set Boundaries Around Perfectionism

Acknowledge that not every decision can be perfect. Most choices can be modified later; what counts is progress, not perfection.

Delegate Where Appropriate

Empower others to make decisions within their areas of responsibility. This not only lightens your load but also builds organisational capability and resilience.

Use the "One-Way/Two-Way Door" Test

Ask: "Is this a reversible decision?" If it is, make it quickly. If not, give it the time it deserves, but commit to a timeline.

Limit Decision Volume

Minimise cognitive load by automating or simplifying routine choices. Establish rituals or frameworks that conserve your mental energy for the most critical decisions.

Building a Culture That Supports Leaders

No leader operates in a vacuum. Organisations must also take responsibility for supporting leaders who are experiencing emotional fatigue or decision paralysis. This means:
- normalising mental health and emotional literacy
- creating safe spaces for vulnerability and support
- balancing accountability with empathy
- providing executive coaching or confidential peer support programs.

Leadership shouldn't come at the expense of wellbeing. When leaders receive emotional and structural support, they make better decisions, demonstrate healthy performance, and lead with clarity and care.

Leading Through Fatigue and Fog

Emotional fatigue and decision paralysis aren't failures; they are signals that something is amiss. They indicate that the human system behind the title is overloaded and requires restoration. Recognising them isn't a weakness but a profound act of leadership.

In an era that demands constant adaptability and resilience, emotionally intelligent leadership involves nurturing one's inner landscape. Leaders must learn to honour their limits, manage their energy, and develop decision-making habits that are sustainable, not heroic.

To lead others effectively, we must first lead ourselves with grace. Sometimes, the bravest decision a leader can make is to pause, breathe, and return to the work rejuvenated, prepared to bear the burden again with steadier hands and a clearer heart.

Personal Reflection: The Cost of Emotional Silence

For years, I believed emotions had no place in leadership. My early experiences in the Army reinforced this belief; we were taught to suppress our feelings, maintain our military bearing, and never let emotions interfere with command. The only emotion that seemed acceptable was anger. Yelling, berating, or intimidating others wasn't just tolerated; they often modelled it in senior positions. I was even told once, "You can't ever disrespect someone you outrank; they can only disrespect you." I internalised that message, and regrettably, there were times when I acted in ways that, in hindsight, I'm not proud of.

Leadership, as I understood it back then, was mostly about administration, knowing where your soldiers came from, who their families were, and where they lived. However, we were rarely encouraged to understand who they truly were beneath the uniform. We weren't allowed to show emotion, and it wasn't safe for them to show it either. Even in the face of tragedy, loss, and pain, we wore masks of stoicism. Everyone could see the hurt, but we didn't dare speak it out loud for fear of appearing weak.

When I left the Army in 2013, what struck me most was how emotionally shattered we all were. After more than a decade at war, many of us were running on empty, exhausted, angry, grieving, and disconnected from ourselves and each other. I carry a quiet sorrow for the friends I've lost since, not to combat but to the invisible weight of unspoken emotion. I often wonder: what might have changed if we had been taught to acknowledge our feelings, to discuss what we felt, and to view vulnerability not as weakness but as a human strength?

Today, I lead very differently. I've learned that emotional connection is not a liability; it's the foundation of trust, resilience, and authentic leadership. Never underestimate the power of making space for people to be seen, heard, and felt. It could be what keeps them going.

PART TWO

The Leader's Emotional Spectrum

Fear and Courage

Leadership is often portrayed as embodying strength, decisiveness, clarity, and confidence. Yet beneath this image lies an often-overlooked truth: leadership frequently involves fear. Fear of the unknown, of failure, of letting others down. It is not the absence of fear that defines outstanding leadership but the courage to lead despite it.

Fear and courage exist in a state of constant tension. Courage does not emerge from certainty but from vulnerability and risk. For leaders, cultivating courage is not just a personal imperative; it is a professional one. Without courage, progress halts. With it, leaders step into the discomfort that transformation requires.

The Nature of Fear

Fear in leadership can manifest in various ways, such as fear of criticism, fear of making the wrong decision, fear of conflict, fear of disappointing others, or even fear of success and the responsibilities that come with it. These fears aren't signs of weakness; instead, they reflect natural human responses to high stakes.

Leaders face constant scrutiny. Their decisions impact livelihoods, reputations, and outcomes. They are expected to strike a balance between vision and realism, optimism and accountability, as well as strength and compassion. This multifaceted role exposes leaders to ongoing risks, both external and internal.

Some fears are situationally linked to specific decisions or crises. Others are more existential, stemming from impostor syndrome or self-doubt. Whatever the source, fear can lead to hesitation, avoidance, or defensiveness if it is not acknowledged and managed.

The Role of Courage

Courage isn't the absence of fear; it's action in the face of fear. In leadership, courage manifests in various ways, such as making unpopular decisions, challenging the status quo, owning up to mistakes, and standing alone when necessary. These acts of bravery often go unnoticed, but they shape culture, build trust, and define legacies.

Displaying courage in leadership requires emotional resilience, along with a clear set of values. Leaders need to question themselves. What do I stand for? What am I willing to risk for what is right? When those answers are clear, courage shifts from being about bravado to emphasising integrity.

Types of Courage

Moral Courage

Standing up for what is right, even when it's unpopular or uncomfortable, involves calling out unethical behaviour, advocating for fairness, and resisting pressure to compromise one's values.

Strategic Courage

Making bold decisions with a long-term vision, even when short-term results are uncertain, is crucial. Leaders who innovate or pivot during uncertainty demonstrate strategic courage.

Emotional Courage

Being vulnerable, seeking feedback, or admitting failure demonstrates courage. This kind of bravery fosters psychological safety and authenticity.

Relational Courage

Engaging in honest conversations, providing constructive feedback, or respectfully confronting conflict builds strong relationships on this foundation.

Fear as a Source of Insight

Instead of being something to avoid, fear can serve as a valuable guide. It reveals where our deepest values reside. A leader who fears failure often values excellence and impact. Conversely, one who fears rejection may genuinely care about connection and a sense of belonging. Fear highlights what truly matters.

When leaders reflect on their fears, they can harness them to enhance self-awareness. Why does this frighten me? What am I safeguarding? What does this reveal about what I value? By confronting fear with curiosity, leaders turn it from an adversary into a mentor.

How Leaders Build Courage

Clarify Your Purpose

A clear sense of purpose grounds courage. When you know what you're fighting for—your mission, your values—you're more likely to act bravely in service of that cause.

Start Small

Courage grows through use. Start by speaking up in a meeting, providing honest feedback, or making a difficult choice without deflection. Each act reinforces the habit.

Surround Yourself with Support

Even courageous leaders require encouragement. A trusted circle of peers or mentors can help you process your fears, offer perspective, and reinforce your confidence and resolve.

Reflect on Past Courage

Remind yourself of the times you've shown bravery in the past. What supported you then? What were the results? These reminders reinforce your identity as a courageous leader.

Accept Discomfort as Growth

Growth and comfort rarely coexist. Courageous leadership involves embracing the discomfort of change, uncertainty, and exposure. This is where transformation begins.

Leading Through Fear

Some of the most profound moments in leadership occur during crises, conflicts, or periods of change. These moments are when fear is at its peak, but so is the potential for growth. Great leaders acknowledge fear, both their own and that of their teams, but don't allow it to dictate their actions.

They demonstrate calm under pressure, as well as humanity. They say, "This is hard. I don't have all the answers. But we'll face this together." This balance of strength and vulnerability fosters trust and resilience.

Leaders also help others navigate fear. They normalise it, provide clarity amid uncertainty, and offer reassurance without false promises. By doing so, they create a space for collective courage.

The Cost of Fearful Leadership

When fear goes unacknowledged or unmanaged, it becomes destructive. Fearful leaders often:
- avoid necessary conversations or decisions
- micromanage to reduce perceived risks
- suppress dissent or innovation
- blame others or deflect responsibility.

This erodes trust, stifles growth, and weakens culture. Over time, organisations run by fear become reactive, inflexible, and risk-averse.

In contrast, courageous leadership fosters environments of accountability, creativity, and empowerment. People feel safe to speak up, try new things, and challenge norms because they see their leader doing the same.

Fear and Courage Are Partners

Fear isn't the enemy of leadership; it's the proving ground. Every courageous act starts with fear. What matters isn't whether fear is present but how we respond to it.

Courageous leaders don't pretend to be fearless. They acknowledge fear, manage it with self-awareness, and act regardless. They cultivate cultures where fear isn't taboo and courage is genuine, not performative. These leaders stand out not because they are immune to fear but because they choose to lead through it, with heart, clarity, and purpose.

Ultimately, courage in leadership is not about being heroic; it's about being human. It involves the quiet decision to do what is right, rather than what is easy. It means showing up time and again in the face of fear and saying, "Let's move forward together."

Fear of Failure, Rejection, and Irrelevance

Behind every leadership decision, presentation, or strategic risk lies a shadow that many seldom discuss openly: the fear of failure, rejection, and irrelevance. These fears often remain concealed behind confident demeanours, polished statements, and decisive actions, yet they are profoundly felt, even by the most seasoned leaders. It tends to be the leaders who care most about people, results, and legacy who experience these fears most acutely.

Understanding these fears is crucial not only for cultivating emotionally intelligent leadership but also for encouraging resilience, self-compassion, and ongoing effectiveness. If left unaddressed, they can influence decisions, distort relationships, and hinder both personal and organisational growth. Conversely, when acknowledged and managed, they can serve as powerful motivators for clarity, authenticity, and courage.

Fear of Failure: The Leader's Silent Burden

Failure is one of the most pervasive fears in leadership. Whether it's the failure of a strategy, a missed target, or a cultural misstep, the stakes for leaders are high. Unlike individual contributors, leaders bear not only personal accountability but also the weight of teams, organisations, and public scrutiny.

Why it's so powerful:

Failure in leadership is seldom private. When things go wrong, people look to the leader for explanations, accountability, and direction. Leaders may internalise this pressure, viewing setbacks not merely as situational but as personal failings. For high-achieving or perfectionist leaders, this fear can become paralysing.

How it shows up:

- Reluctance to innovate or take bold action.
- Over-cautious strategies that prioritise safety over impact
- Harsh self-criticism or perfectionism
- Blaming external factors or avoiding ownership

Healthy reframing:

Failure isn't the opposite of success; it's part of the journey towards it. Resilient leaders learn to view failure as data, not as a reflection of their identity. They ask, "What did we learn? What will we do differently next time?" Leaders who model this mindset foster cultures where experimentation and reflection are valued more than perfection.

Fear of Rejection: The Hidden Cost of Visibility

Leadership often involves stepping into the spotlight, speaking publicly, challenging others, standing by decisions, or expressing unpopular views. With this visibility comes the risk of rejection: of being disliked, dismissed, misunderstood, or excluded. For many leaders, particularly those driven by a desire for connection or validation, this fear can be a quietly consuming one.

Why it's so powerful:

Human beings are wired for belonging, and leaders are no exception. The fear of rejection taps into our primal need to be accepted. In leadership, this becomes complicated by the political and interpersonal dynamics of teams, boards, communities, or the public. A leader's decisions will rarely please everyone, and that discomfort can be difficult to bear.

How it shows up:
- People-pleasing behaviour or over-accommodation
- Avoidance of hard conversations or controversial positions
- Seeking validation at the expense of principle
- Difficulty delegating or giving honest feedback

Healthy reframing:

Being rejected is not always a sign of failure. At times, rejection indicates that a leader is challenging their comfort zone, pushing back against groupthink, or holding firm to their values. Courageous leadership sometimes involves disappointing people to stay aligned with a greater purpose. Leaders must learn to distinguish between being liked and being respected.

Fear of Irrelevance: The Quiet Anxiety of Obsolescence

Perhaps the most existential of leadership fears is that of irrelevance. As industries evolve, teams change, and new talent emerges, many leaders quietly wonder: Will I be needed tomorrow? Will I still matter? Will I keep up? This fear often arises later in a career, especially as younger generations bring different skills, values, and expectations to the workplace.

Why it's so powerful:

For many, leadership becomes a core part of their identity. Losing influence or being passed over isn't just a professional concern; it strikes at the heart of self-worth. In rapidly changing environments, the pace of technological change or cultural shifts can feel like a threat to one's relevance.

How it shows up:

- Clinging to past successes or legacy practices
- Resistance to change, new ideas, or generational input
- Defensive behaviour when challenged or corrected
- Over-identification with titles or authority

Healthy reframing:

Relevance isn't about being the most intelligent person in the room; it's about being adaptive, curious, and open. Leaders stay relevant by being teachable, mentoring others, and evolving with their industries. Humility and curiosity serve as the antidotes to irrelevance. When leaders create space for others to shine, they often shine brighter in the process.

Intersections and Impact

These three fears are often interconnected. A leader who is afraid of failure may also fear rejection if the team or board loses confidence in them. A leader fearing irrelevance might avoid innovation or collaboration to protect their perceived value. The cumulative impact of these fears can lead to:

- decision paralysis
- emotional fatigue

- diminished authenticity
- breakdowns in trust and communication.

Moreover, these fears can shape entire organisational cultures. Teams often take emotional cues from their leaders. When fear dominates a leader's inner life, it creates an undercurrent of anxiety, control, and rigidity throughout the system. Conversely, when a leader openly addresses fear and models courage, it fosters a culture of transparency, risk-taking, and trust.

How to Lead Through Fear

Name the Fear

Fear thrives in silence. The first step is to name what you're feeling. "I'm afraid this might fail. I'm nervous about how they'll react." Naming fear doesn't make you weak; it makes you real.

Disentangle Identity from Outcome

Your success rate doesn't define your value. Leadership is a role you fill, not the sum of your worth. When leaders separate their identity from their performance, they become more resilient and grounded.

Surround Yourself with Truth-Tellers

Trusted advisors, mentors, or peers can help reality-check your fears. They provide perspective, affirmation, and the occasional necessary nudge. Don't go it alone.

Reframe Fear as Data

Fear signals something important: a risk, a value, a potential loss. Ask yourself, "What is this fear trying to protect? What's the opportunity within it?" Use fear to inform, not control, your decisions.

Build Habits of Confidence

Confidence isn't a fixed trait; it's a muscle. Build it through practice: small acts of courage, consistent learning, and celebrating progress, not just perfection.

Fear Is Human; Courage Is a Choice

Fear of failure, rejection, and irrelevance is part of the leadership journey. These fears may never entirely disappear, and that's okay. What matters is how we respond to them. Do we let them shrink our vision, soften our voice, and stall our growth? Or do we meet them with curiosity, self-awareness, and courage?

Speaking the Truth, Taking Risks, and Being Vulnerable

Leadership isn't just about directing teams or making decisions; it's about being authentic in the face of complexity. At its most potent, leadership relies on truth, risk, and vulnerability. These three qualities can feel uncomfortable, particularly in environments that prioritise control, certainty, and authority. Yet they are precisely what distinguishes transactional managers from transformational leaders.

Truth, risk, and vulnerability are not merely add-ons to leadership; they are at its core. They build trust, cultivate authenticity, and create the conditions for growth. However, embracing them requires courage. To lead in this manner is to reject comfort and choose integrity, even when the stakes are high.

Speaking the Truth: Leadership Built on Integrity

Truth-telling in leadership is a discipline. It's not merely about being factually correct; it's about being honest in communication, consistent in values, and transparent in intent. Speaking the truth involves saying what needs to be said, even when it's difficult, unpopular, or uncomfortable.

Why leaders avoid it:
- fear of conflict or damaging relationships
- worry about loss of reputation or backlash
- doubts about timing or consequences
- pressure to maintain a positive image or morale.

But when the truth is avoided, the consequences are worse:
- problems go unaddressed
- mistrust grows
- teams operate on false assumptions
- culture becomes characterised by avoidance and silence.

Truth-telling in practice includes:
- giving constructive feedback with clarity and care
- naming risks or issues that others won't
- owning up to mistakes and limitations
- communicating organisational challenges honestly without sugar-coating.

Leaders who speak the truth demonstrate that honesty is valued more than perfection. They foster environments where others feel safe to speak up, challenge ideas, and bring their whole selves to the table.

Taking Risks: Leadership as a Bold Act

Leadership is inherently risky. Every decision, every stance, and every act of innovation or dissent carries the potential for failure, criticism, or loss. However, without risk, there is no growth. Leaders who shun risk create stagnant systems, while those who embrace it—thoughtfully and courageously—propel people and ideas forward.

Risks in leadership come in many forms such as:
- introducing an untested idea
- promoting an unconventional team member
- challenging powerful stakeholders
- changing long-held traditions or processes
- speaking out against injustice or dysfunction.

Why risk is difficult

Risk challenges the safety of what we know. It invites scrutiny and exposes us to vulnerability. Yet all progress in leadership comes from someone willing to say, "There's a better way, and I'm eager to go first."

Risk is not the same as recklessness. Effective leaders balance boldness with judgement. They prepare, consult, and reflect; ultimately, they act. They understand that delaying indefinitely for perfect certainty is itself a risk of missed opportunities, eroding trust, and becoming irrelevant.

Being Vulnerable: The Strength in Showing Humanity

Among all the traits often misunderstood in leadership, vulnerability is arguably the most powerful and the most misrepresented. It's not about weakness, oversharing, or emotional impulsivity. Vulnerability involves the courage to be seen, to lead without masks, to admit limitations, to ask for help, and to acknowledge uncertainty.

Brené Brown[4] defines vulnerability as "uncertainty, risk, and emotional exposure." In leadership, this might look like:
- saying "I don't know" in front of your team
- admitting a mistake publicly

---

4. (Brown, *Daring greatly: How the courage to be vulnerable transforms the way we live, love, parent and lead*, 2012)

- giving a heartfelt apology
- sharing the emotional reality of a tough decision
- asking for feedback, knowing it may be difficult to hear.

Why vulnerability matters:
- It humanises leaders and builds a connection.
- It fosters psychological safety, where others feel free to be open and honest.
- It models accountability and humility.
- It strengthens resilience, because leaders no longer have to pretend to be invincible.

Why it's hard

We've been conditioned to equate leadership with stoicism and control. Vulnerability challenges that narrative. It requires trusting that your value as a leader isn't diminished by showing emotion or imperfection; it's deepened by it.

The Interdependence of Truth, Risk, and Vulnerability

These three qualities are not separate; they are intertwined.
- Speaking the truth often requires vulnerability, especially when that truth is complicated.
- Taking a risk involves telling the truth about what needs to change and accepting the vulnerability of exposure if it fails.
- Vulnerability, when practised with intention, leads to more profound truth and a greater willingness to risk authenticity over appearance.

When these qualities are consistently embodied, leaders become more trustworthy, approachable, and inspiring. Teams understand that it is safe to speak honestly, to take risks and possibly fail, and to show up as whole individuals, not just competent performers.

Organisational Impact of Courageous Leadership

Leaders who embody truth, risk-taking, and vulnerability have a profound impact on culture. Their teams are:
- more innovative, because the fear of failure is reduced
- more engaged, because people feel seen and heard
- more resilient, because honesty builds alignment and trust
- more ethical, because transparency is valued over convenience.

On the contrary, organisations where these qualities are missing often experience:
- passive cultures where silence replaces accountability
- resistance to change and fear of innovation
- high levels of stress and disengagement
- leadership fatigue from the pressure of emotional concealment.

Culture reflects leadership. When leaders share hard truths, take genuine risks, and reveal their humanity, others are more inclined to follow suit. This leads to an organisation characterised by integrity, creativity, and a sense of purpose.

How Leaders Can Cultivate These Traits

Start with Self-Reflection

Ask yourself: "What truths am I avoiding? What risks am I hesitating to take? Where am I withholding vulnerability?" Self-awareness is the first act of courage.

Model Transparency in Small Moments

You don't need grand speeches. Acknowledging a challenge, thanking someone for tough feedback, or stating, "This is difficult," are simple ways to foster a culture of openness.

Create Safe Spaces for Truth

Encourage honest feedback, and acknowledge it. Safeguard those who raise concerns. Express gratitude when individuals share uncomfortable truths.

Celebrate Smart Risks and Honest Failures

Normalise failure as a part of the learning process. When something doesn't go as planned, discuss openly what was learned. This removes shame and fosters experimentation.

Share the "Why" Behind Vulnerability

Let people know why you're being open. "I'm sharing this because I want us to learn together." This helps people understand that being vulnerable is purposeful, not performative.

Leading With an Open Heart

Leadership that speaks the truth, takes risks, and embraces vulnerability isn't easy, but it's essential. In a complex world filled with performance pressures and noise, people yearn for genuine leaders. Leaders who will tell the truth even when it costs them. Leaders who will take risks not to prove themselves but to improve the world. Leaders who will say, "I don't have all the answers, but I'm here with you anyway."

Truth, risk, and vulnerability aren't just traits to layer onto your leadership; they form the foundation for creating a lasting impact. They're not merely strategies, but commitments—to people, to progress, and to purpose.

And when leaders live these commitments with courage, they do more than lead; they inspire.

The best leaders are not fearless; they are those who feel fear yet move forward, anchored in purpose, guided by values, and committed to truth. They do not lead from a desire to be perfect but from a willingness to be present. In doing so, they don't just lead organisations; they lead people, with humanity and heart.

Doubt and Conviction

Leadership is often framed as the realm of certainty: having a clear vision, making confident decisions, and inspiring others to follow. Yet beneath even the most resolute leadership lies an internal dance between doubt and conviction. These two forces are not opposites in conflict but companions in balance. Great leaders are not those who have eliminated doubt but those who learn to lead through it, anchored by conviction and tempered by humility.

Understanding and navigating the interplay of doubt and conviction is essential for responsible, resilient, and effective leadership. When managed effectively, doubt fuels reflection and learning, while conviction offers the clarity and courage to act.

The Presence of Doubt in Leadership

Doubt in leadership is natural and necessary. The complexity, visibility, and high stakes of leadership make absolute certainty rare. Doubt emerges in moments of ambiguity, when information is incomplete or outcomes are unpredictable. It arises at strategic forks, ethical dilemmas, or crises where no path is entirely correct.

Healthy doubt prompts introspection. Am I missing something? Have I consulted the right people? Am I acting in alignment with our values? It opens the door to better questions, deeper listening, and more inclusive decision-making.

However, unmanaged doubt can undermine confidence. It can result in hesitation, second-guessing, or avoidance. When leaders overlook and fail to address doubt, they may appear indecisive or out of touch, thereby diminishing their influence and credibility.

The Role of Conviction

Conviction, in contrast, is the inner certainty that sustains a leader through difficulty. It is grounded in purpose, values, and vision. While doubt asks, "Are we sure?", conviction answers, "This is what matters."

Conviction enables decisive action in uncertainty. It offers moral and strategic clarity. It is the engine behind bold decisions, cultural change, and long-term vision. Leaders with conviction are not reckless; they are anchored. They know what they stand for, and that knowledge helps guide others through complexity.

Importantly, conviction isn't about being right all the time; it's about being committed to doing what is right, even when the outcome is unclear. It's not stubbornness; it's integrity.

The Tension: Doubt Without Conviction, Conviction Without Doubt

Without conviction, doubt leads to paralysis. Leaders flounder, chasing consensus or shirking responsibility. Their teams feel uncertain and unsupported.

Without doubt, conviction can turn into arrogance. Leaders may act without reflection, dismiss feedback, and reinforce flawed ideas. This can lead to blind spots, ethical lapses, or cultural damage.

Effective leadership holds both in tension:
- Doubt invites questioning: are we seeing this?
- Conviction asserts: we must move forward anyway.

The most trusted leaders are those who express humble conviction. They acknowledge what they don't know, seek input, and still provide direction. They say, "This is hard. There are risks. But here's what I believe we need to do."

How Leaders Can Manage Doubt Constructively

Recognise Doubt as a Signal

Instead of suppressing doubt, use it as an opportunity to pause and reflect. Is there something being overlooked? Are you navigating unfamiliar territory? Is there a lack of alignment?

Seek Diverse Perspectives

Invite a challenge. Bring in others with different perspectives or expertise to broaden your understanding. Doubt can signal the need to expand your viewpoint.

Clarify the Decision-Making Framework

Doubt often arises when decisions appear unclear or uncertain. What are your criteria? What are the non-negotiables? Having a framework helps separate emotion from reasoning.

Practice Self-Awareness

Not all doubt is rational. Some arise from fear, fatigue, or past wounds. Be aware when your inner critic is louder than your rational voice.

Use Reflective Questions
- What am I afraid will happen if I get this wrong?
- Who am I trying to protect? Myself, the organisation, or the team?
- What values are at stake?

These questions turn doubt into direction.

How Leaders Cultivate Conviction

Know Your Values
Conviction stems from a clear set of values. Leaders need to understand what they stand for and why they do. This moral clarity enables them to make tough decisions with consistency and integrity.

Stay Anchored in Purpose
When circumstances change, purpose stays constant. Leaders with conviction continually return to why they do what they do. Purpose provides meaning to risk and instils resilience against doubt.

Communicate Transparently
People want to follow leaders who are genuine and authentic. Share your thought process. Let them see that your decisions are based on principle, not ego.

Reinforce Commitment with Action
Conviction is strengthened when it aligns with consistent behaviour. Each act of integrity reinforces belief in yourself and others' trust in you.

The Inner Dialogue: Leading Yourself First

Leadership involves constant inner dialogue:

- Do I know what I'm doing?
- What if this goes wrong?
- Am I still the right person for this role?

These questions are not signs of weak leadership; they're signs of self-awareness. Leaders must learn to lead themselves through doubt with compassion and clarity. This means recognising fear but not being ruled by it. It involves reminding yourself of past strengths, current values, and future goals.

Conviction without introspection is dangerous. Doubt without courage is immobilising. However, together, they foster wise, adaptive, and human leadership.

Modelling Doubt and Conviction to Others

The way leaders manage doubt and conviction communicates signals throughout the organisation. Leaders who display thoughtful self-questioning followed by decisive action cultivate cultures of both critical thinking and forward momentum.

They normalise learning. They demonstrate that uncertainty does not preclude progress. They say, "I considered many views. I had questions. But I believe this is the right path. Let's go." This fosters buy-in and resilience.

Such modelling also empowers emerging leaders. It teaches them that self-doubt is not a disqualifier and that courage often feels like pushing ahead despite uncertainty.

Leading with Both Head and Heart

Doubt and conviction are not opposing forces to be resolved but complementary forces to be harnessed and leveraged. Doubt sharpens conviction, while conviction guides doubt. Together, they foster thoughtful, agile, and principled leadership.

The most effective leaders aren't those who silence doubt or cling unthinkingly to certainty. They are the ones who listen to doubt with humility, respond with courage, and act from a place of grounded integrity.

Leadership, at its core, is the ability to navigate ambiguity while providing clarity and direction. It involves the art of making room for questions while committing to answers. It represents the lifelong discipline of leading with both head and heart.

Navigating Impostor Syndrome

Impostor syndrome is a quiet yet powerful undercurrent in many leadership journeys. Despite achieving external success, recognition, or accomplishments, a surprising number of leaders grapple with a persistent inner voice that whispers, "You're not good enough. You don't belong here. One day, they'll find out you're a fraud".

This experience, known as impostor syndrome, is widespread, even among the most seasoned and accomplished individuals. For leaders, the stakes are even higher. The expectations of control, clarity, and confidence often contrast sharply with the vulnerability and self-doubt they may feel internally. If left unexamined, impostor syndrome can erode trust, distort judgement, and create emotional fatigue. However, when understood and managed, it can transform into a powerful opportunity for growth, self-awareness, and authenticity.

What Is Impostor Syndrome?

Imposter syndrome refers to the internal experience of believing that you are not as capable as others perceive you to be. It's characterised by persistent self-doubt, fear of being exposed, and the belief that achievements stem from luck, timing, or external assistance, rather than personal ability.

It's important to note that impostor syndrome is not a clinical diagnosis; it's a pattern of thought. While it affects people across all industries and roles, it's particularly pronounced in high-achieving, high-pressure environments, such as leadership.

Why Leaders Are Susceptible

Leaders often find themselves in situations where they must make tough decisions with insufficient information, juggle multiple priorities, and communicate with assurance, even in times of uncertainty. The visibility and accountability that come with leadership roles heighten the fear of failure or being "found out."

Some contributing factors include:
- promotion into new, unfamiliar roles
- being a minority in terms of gender, race, age, or background
- comparisons to predecessors or peers
- high performance standards or perfectionist tendencies
- little or no feedback (or only criticism).

Even capable leaders may feel as though they don't "deserve" their position or that their success is precarious and transient.

Common Thought Patterns of Impostor Syndrome

Discounting Success:
"That project only succeeded because the team worked hard, not because of me."

Attributing Achievements to Luck or Timing:
"I was just in the right place at the right time."

Fear of Exposure:
"Any day now, they'll realise I'm not as good as they think."

Perfectionism:
"If I make one mistake, they'll see I'm a fraud."

Downplaying Capability:
"I don't have the same skills or experience as others in this room."

These internal narratives can undermine leadership by fostering hesitation, a lack of confidence, and the avoidance of high-stakes opportunities.

The Cost of Impostor Syndrome

Unchecked impostor syndrome can have a wide-ranging impact:

- *Burnout*: Constantly trying to "prove yourself" leads to exhaustion.
- *Risk aversion*: Fear of being wrong leads to overly cautious leadership.
- *Stalled growth*: Leaders may avoid promotions, speaking engagements, or other opportunities for visibility.
- *Disconnection*: Emotional distance from teams or colleagues to avoid vulnerability.
- *Overcompensation*: Micromanaging or overcontrolling in an attempt to mask insecurity.

Perhaps most damaging, impostor syndrome can prevent leaders from truly enjoying their roles. Achievements feel hollow. Relationships feel performative. Work transforms into a stage instead of remaining a place of service and impact.

Breaking the Cycle: How Leaders Can Navigate Imposter Syndrome

Name It Without Shame

The first step is to recognise and normalise the experience. Many leaders feel isolated in their self-doubt, but the truth is that impostor syndrome affects a wide range of high performers. Saying, "I'm experiencing impostor feelings," helps to detach identity from the experience.

Separate Feelings from Facts

Feelings are genuine, but they aren't always dependable. Just because you feel like a fraud doesn't mean you are one. Record your achievements. Reflect on your qualifications. Ask yourself, "What evidence do I have for or against this belief?"

Practice Self-Compassion

Instead of criticising yourself for self-doubt, greet it with kindness. Say, "It's okay to feel this way. This is hard, and I'm doing my best." Self-compassion boosts resilience and alleviates the shame that fuels impostor syndrome.

Talk to Trusted Allies

Talk about your feelings with a mentor, coach, or peer. You'll likely find that others have experienced similar emotions. Supportive conversations can reshape your narrative and remind you of your strengths.

Redefine Success

Perfectionism fosters impostor syndrome. Redefine success as learning, growth, or impact, not flawlessness. Are you creating value? Are you showing up with integrity? These measures are more sustainable and fulfilling.

Celebrate Progress, Not Just Outcomes

Leadership is a journey, not a test. Recognise the moments of courage, clarity, or improvement, even when the outcome isn't perfect. This fosters internal validation and diminishes dependence on external praise.

The Power of Vulnerability in Overcoming Impostor Syndrome

One of the most counterintuitive yet effective ways to tackle impostor syndrome is by being vulnerable. When leaders openly acknowledge uncertainty, seek input, or share their learning journey, they demonstrate that it's alright not to have all the answers.

Vulnerability fosters connection. It demonstrates to others that leadership isn't about being infallible; instead, it's about being responsible, honest, and responsive. Leaders who embrace vulnerability often notice that the fear of exposure diminishes, as they no longer attempt to maintain a flawless façade.

Reclaiming Authority from Within

Ultimately, navigating impostor syndrome involves shifting your locus of control or locus of validation. Instead of depending on titles, applause, or comparisons, you start to cultivate internal trust, believing in your judgement, values, and voice.

Ask yourself:
- What do I know to be true about myself?
- What values guide me?
- What impact do I want to create?

- What kind of leader do I choose to be?

These questions create an inner compass that steadies you when impostor feelings arise.

You Belong Because You Show Up

Impostor syndrome isn't a disqualifier; it's a sign that you care. It indicates that you take your role seriously. However, you don't need to be perfect to be powerful. You don't need to silence self-doubt to speak with conviction. Instead, you need to keep showing up, authentically, courageously, and with a commitment to growth.

The leaders who endure are not those who silence every fear but those who learn to carry self-doubt gently, without allowing it to hold them back. They lead not because they feel ready every day but because they understand that the mission matters more than a moment of fear.

You are not an impostor. You are a leader learning in real time, and that is enough.

Building Trust in Your Judgement

At the heart of effective leadership lies a quiet, internal force: trust in one's judgement. While strategy, data, collaboration, and advice are essential in leadership, there comes a moment in every leader's journey when the final decision must be made. And in that moment, when ambiguity is high, consensus is elusive, and consequences are real, the leader must rely on their discernment.

Trusting your judgement isn't about being certain, infallible, or unshakably confident. It's about cultivating a grounded belief that your thought process is sound, your values are clear, and your intent aligns with the greater good. It serves as an internal compass, a form of self-leadership, that enables wise, timely, and courageous decisions.

Why Trust in Judgement Matters

Without trust in their judgement, leaders falter. They overly rely on consensus, seek constant reassurance, or delay making critical decisions. They become reactive rather than proactive. Over time, this erodes their credibility, not because they make mistakes, but because they seem indecisive, uncertain, or disconnected.

On the other hand, leaders who trust their judgement create clarity and momentum. They weigh evidence and insights, listen to others, and then act with resolve. Even when the path is uncertain, their steady presence builds confidence in those around them.

More importantly, trusting your judgement shields you from the chaos of external pressure. It enables you to act from principle rather than popularity, ensuring that your leadership remains anchored when the storm hits.

Why Leaders Struggle to Trust Themselves

Fear of Getting It Wrong

Leadership decisions often have high stakes. Fear of failure or negative consequences can cause leaders to second-guess themselves, even when their instincts are sound.

Overexposure to External Voices

Leaders, surrounded by consultants, advisors, boards, and stakeholders, can easily become overwhelmed by the multitude of inputs. While diverse perspectives are essential, excessive noise can obscure internal clarity.

Perfectionism or Imposter Syndrome

Leaders who believe they must have everything perfect or who doubt their legitimacy are more inclined to defer to others or shirk decisive action.

Past Mistakes or Criticism

Experiences of failure or public criticism can foster self-doubt, particularly if those moments were never fully processed or reinterpreted as learning opportunities.

What Trusting Your Judgement Looks Like
- You seek advice but are not dependent on it.
- You know when to wait and when to move.
- You make peace with imperfection, choosing progress over paralysis.
- You are willing to make the hard call, even when others disagree.
- You reflect and refine your thinking without undermining your authority.

Trusting your judgement is not ego; it is disciplined self-assurance. It is built on rigorous thought, self-awareness, and a consistent decision-making process.

How to Build Trust in Your Judgement

Strengthen Self-Awareness
Start by understanding your patterns, triggers, and tendencies. Reflect on questions like:
- What situations make me doubt myself?
- When have I made decisions I'm proud of?
- What thought patterns emerge when I'm under pressure?

Self-awareness helps you recognise when your inner critic is dominating and when your intuition is attempting to communicate.

Clarify Your Values and Principles
The most trustworthy judgement is values-driven. When you understand what you stand for—integrity, fairness, courage, and service—you establish a decision-making compass that surpasses trends or opinions.

Ask yourself:
- What matters most in this situation?
- What would I decide if I removed fear or ego?
- What decision aligns with long-term wellbeing, not just short-term relief?

Develop and Refine a Decision-Making Framework

Instead of winging it, use a consistent process:
- Define the decision clearly.
- Gather relevant facts and insights.
- Seek diverse input.
- Weigh risks and opportunities.
- Consider ethical implications.
- Reflect on your intuition.
- Decide and communicate clearly.
- Review outcomes and learn from them.

This repeatable process fosters confidence and clarity over time. It establishes a track record that affirms your ability to lead thoughtfully and effectively.

Learn from Mistakes; Don't Fear Them

No leader makes perfect decisions. The goal is not flawlessness but learning. When a decision doesn't go as planned, please resist the urge to internalise it as a failure. Instead:
- analyse what went wrong
- identify what was within your control
- adjust your approach
- reaffirm your commitment to thoughtful leadership.

Every mistake you handle effectively enhances your ability to trust yourself in the future.

Maintain a Reflective Practice

Leaders who take time to think rather than react cultivate a deeper trust in their inner voice. Whether it's journalling, walking, meditating, or chatting with a coach, make space to reflect on your thoughts.

Ask:
- What is my gut telling me?
- What are the risks of waiting versus acting?
- If I were advising someone else, what would I recommend?

Reflection turns reactive leadership into intentional leadership.

Balancing Internal and External Voices

Trusting your judgement doesn't mean ignoring others. Great leaders integrate external feedback with internal clarity. They seek input, listen attentively, and then weigh that feedback against their sense of what is right.

Sometimes, people will push back. That's a good thing; it challenges your thinking. But ultimately, the decision is yours. When you trust your process and your values, you can make bold choices with humility and determination.

The Role of Confidence and Humility

Self-trust is a blend of confidence and humility:
- ***Confidence***: "I have enough experience, insight, and integrity to lead."
- ***Humility***: "I don't know everything, and I'm open to growth."

Leaders who embody both qualities are magnetic. They are trusted because they do not pretend to be perfect. They are credible because they don't waver with every opinion. They listen, reflect, make decisions, and take responsibility.

Modelling Trusted Judgement for Others

When leaders demonstrate trust in their judgement, they teach others to do the same. They model:
- disciplined decision-making
- emotional regulation
- the ability to learn from outcomes
- integrity in action.

This creates a ripple effect. Teams feel more empowered. The culture grows more resilient. And the organisation becomes more agile as people trust both their leaders and themselves.

Leading from the Inside Out

Trusting your judgement isn't about being right every time; it's about staying grounded. It involves leading from a place of alignment, not anxiety, and clarity, not chaos.

You build trust one decision at a time by showing up, reflecting, listening, acting, and learning. The more you practise thoughtful, values-aligned decision making, the stronger your internal trust becomes.

Ultimately, leadership isn't just about guiding others; it's about stewarding yourself. When you learn to trust the leader within, you become the type of leader that others want to follow.

Joy and Fulfilment

Leadership is often framed in terms of responsibility, pressure, and sacrifice, and rightly so. Yet this narrative, while true, is incomplete. At its best, leadership is also a source of deep joy and genuine fulfilment. It offers moments of connection, pride, inspiration, and meaning that few other roles can provide. Amid the challenges, setbacks, and long hours, there is also profound satisfaction in knowing that you are making a difference, guiding others, and building something that truly matters.

Joy and fulfilment are not luxuries reserved for rare moments of success; they are essential to sustainable leadership. They provide the energy to persevere, the clarity to lead with heart, and the resilience to endure. Recognising and nurturing these positive dimensions is key not only to effective leadership but also to a life well lived.

The Nature of Joy

Joy in leadership isn't about constant happiness or superficial optimism. It's about experiencing moments of genuine connection with your work, your team, and your purpose. It can arise unexpectedly, in a chat with a colleague, the successful launch of a project, or witnessing someone you've mentored thrive.

Joy emerges when a leader is aligned with their values, actions, and the impact they have on others. It often occurs when:
- a hard-won decision yields positive outcomes
- a team member grows into their potential
- a shared challenge is overcome through collaboration
- purpose and performance come together.

These moments may not always grab headlines, but they are emotionally rich and meaningful. They renew a leader's sense of purpose and help counterbalance the pressures of leadership's demands.

Fulfilment Through Contribution

True fulfilment in leadership doesn't stem from titles, accolades, or authority. Instead, it arises from contribution. Fulfilment is grounded in the understanding that your work creates a positive impact on people, organisations, and communities.

Leaders experience fulfilment when they:
- create environments where people thrive
- enable change that improves lives
- build cultures of integrity and care
- know that their presence makes a difference.

Fulfilment is cumulative. It builds over time, shaped by small moments of service, connection, and alignment with purpose. It doesn't require external validation, although recognition is welcome; it is sustained by the leader's internal sense of worth and value.

How Leaders Can Cultivate Joy and Fulfilment

Celebrate Small Wins

Too often, leaders rush from one challenge to the next without taking a moment to appreciate their progress. Create opportunities to celebrate small victories, individual milestones, improved relationships, or quiet acts of excellence. These moments nurture joy and reinforce a sense of meaning.

Invest in Relationships

The joy of leadership is profoundly relational. Leading isn't merely about driving performance; it's about fostering trust, connection, and a shared purpose. Take the time to connect with your team, understand their stories, and share your own. Human connection is a rich source of leadership fulfilment.

Align Work with Purpose

When your daily tasks feel connected to a larger mission, joy becomes more accessible. Revisit your purpose regularly. Ask, "Why does this matter? Who benefits from this work? What legacy am I building?"

Purpose transforms routine into meaning.

Practice Gratitude

Gratitude helps leaders shift from what's missing to what's meaningful. Regularly acknowledge the people and moments that bring you joy. Gratitude also fosters humility and appreciation, two quiet yet powerful drivers of fulfilment.

Honour Your Strengths

Fulfilment comes from using your strengths in service of others. Identify what energises you, whether it's visioning, mentoring, problem-solving, or creating. Seek out opportunities to engage in what brings you alive within your leadership role.

Joy as a Leadership Asset

Leaders who embrace joy are not naïve; they are resilient. Joy is not the absence of struggle; it is the presence of hope and appreciation amid that struggle. It sustains energy and morale. It's contagious. A joyful leader elevates the emotional tone of the team, creating an environment in which others can thrive.

Joyful leadership encourages creativity and innovation. When people feel safe, valued, and inspired, they are more likely to take risks, share ideas, and genuinely collaborate. Joy acts as a catalyst, not a distraction, for high performance.

Fulfilment as an Antidote to Burnout

Leadership burnout is a genuine issue, especially in high-stakes or mission-driven environments. Fulfilment serves as one of the most substantial buffers against it. When leaders feel fulfilled, they are more likely to persevere through challenges, recover from setbacks, and lead sustainably.

Fulfilment also reduces the tendency to chase external markers of success, such as status, power, and control, which, while sometimes gratifying, do not sustain long-term wellbeing. A fulfilled leader leads from a place of inner abundance, not scarcity.

Barriers to Joy and Fulfilment

Despite its importance, many leaders struggle to experience joy and fulfilment.

Some reasons include:

- *Chronic busyness*: When every moment is scheduled, there's no space to notice or appreciate the good.

- ***Perfectionism***: The belief that nothing is ever "good enough" robs leaders of the ability to celebrate or feel satisfied.
- ***Emotional detachment***: Some leaders armour themselves emotionally to manage pressure. But numbing pain also numbs joy.
- ***External focus***: When leadership is overly focused on outcomes, numbers, and optics, the human side, the source of genuine joy, is often overlooked.

Overcoming these barriers requires intention. Leaders must choose to slow down, reflect, and re-engage with the heart of their work.

Leadership That Radiates Joy

Leaders who find joy in what they do radiate energy, inspiration, and authenticity. They are more likely to:
- attract and retain talent
- build high-trust, high-performance cultures
- inspire others to find meaning in their work
- model emotional maturity and resilience.

These leaders acknowledge the challenge, but they refuse to let it dictate their experience. They strike a balance between gravity and lightness, seriousness and play, strength and soul.

Leading With Joy, Living with Fulfilment

Joy and fulfilment in leadership are not mere side effects; they are indicators. They signal that we are in the right place, engaging in work that matters, in ways that align with who we are.

To lead with joy is not to lead without pain. It is to stay open, to emotion, to connection, to the human spirit at work.

To lead with fulfilment is to know that your efforts mean something beyond results. It is to look back on the journey, not just with pride but with a quiet sense of gratitude. I was part of something that mattered. And it changed me, too.

The Highs of Achievement and Team Success

Leadership is often described as a weight, a responsibility to carry, a duty to fulfil, a burden to bear. Yet alongside that weight, leadership also offers highs—moments of triumph, shared achievement, and team success that can be deeply energising and affirming. These are the moments when the effort pays off, when a vision becomes reality, and when a group of individuals becomes something more than the sum of its parts.

The highs of leadership aren't just about personal accolades or achieving performance targets; they are about fostering a culture of excellence. They're about collective momentum, shared victories, and the powerful emotional reward of witnessing a team surmount challenges together. These highs matter. They inspire perseverance, strengthen team bonds, and remind leaders why they are in leadership positions.

The Nature of Achievement

Achievement in leadership is rarely a solitary pursuit. Even individual recognitions, such as promotions, awards, or praise, often stem from the success of a team or organisation.

Consequently, leadership achievement is relational and systemic. It arises from:
- delivering results that create a positive impact
- guiding a team through uncertainty toward a shared goal
- seeing people grow, thrive, and succeed under your leadership
- completing a complex project, overcoming obstacles, and reaching milestones.

Achievement isn't just about winning. It's about creating movement, realising purpose, and bringing people together to do something meaningful.

The Emotional Highs of Success

There is a unique emotional intensity that comes with shared success.
- Relief after a long effort.
- Joy in recognition of collective effort.
- Pride in the team's growth and resilience.
- Gratitude for having contributed something enduring.
- Connection to others who were part of the journey.

These emotions aren't fleeting. They leave a lasting mark. Leaders often remember not just the moment of success but also the people who stood beside them, the shared laughter, the struggles, the sacrifices, and the final celebrations. These memories fuel a sense of purpose long after the task is done.

Celebrating Team Success: More Than Just a Gesture

One of the most essential roles of a leader is to acknowledge and amplify the team's success. Celebration is not just a "nice to have"; it's a leadership responsibility. It reinforces effort, strengthens culture, and builds motivation.

Effective leaders:
- acknowledge individual and team contributions specifically
- create space for celebration, even in busy or high-pressure environments
- share credit freely.
- share the success story, emphasising the challenges overcome.
- connect success with values and purpose.

When celebration is genuine and inclusive, it creates emotional resonance. People feel acknowledged, valued, and connected. This, in turn, fosters loyalty and drives future performance.

The Role of Achievement in Leader Identity

While fulfilment and meaning are vital to long-term leadership wellbeing, achievement still plays a crucial role in identity. Leaders often gain confidence and affirmation from tangible results. Achievements validate vision, justify tough decisions, and confirm that one's leadership is making an impact.

However, it's crucial to anchor achievement in process, not just outcome. When leaders attach their identity solely to wins, they risk emotional volatility, feeling elated in success and unworthy in failure. The healthiest leaders regard achievement as confirmation of good work, rather than the sole source of self-worth.

What Success Feels Like for a Leader

Success for a leader is often layered:
- ***Professional satisfaction***: a feeling that the strategy was effective and the goals were achieved.

- **Personal pride**: recognition that your intuition, courage, or effort has made a difference.
- **Relational connection**: a shared emotion with the team that fosters a sense of unity.
- **Renewed purpose**: energy to keep going and lead into the following challenge.

These feelings are not selfish. When embraced with humility and shared generously, they deepen a leader's effectiveness and authenticity.

The Power of Shared Effort and Collective Victory

The most satisfying leadership highs are not solo moments; they are shared experiences. The culmination of months of collaboration, challenges, and collective effort creates a bond that endures long after the task is completed. These moments build trust, culture, and identity.

When teams succeed together, they:
- develop mutual respect through shared struggle
- build confidence in one another's capabilities
- strengthen psychological safety through mutual support
- celebrate not just the "what" but the "how" of success.

As a leader, facilitating these experiences is one of the most powerful things you can do to support your team. You're not just leading towards results; you're building a community of achievement.

Sustaining Momentum After the High

One of the challenges that follows a major success is "now what?" syndrome. After months of intense activity, leaders and teams can experience a post-achievement lull. Leaders must be deliberate in sustaining energy while allowing space for rest and reflection.

Ways to navigate the post-success moment:
- ***Pause and reflect***: Ask, "What did we learn? What made this successful?"
- ***Document and share***: Capture the story of the achievement to inspire others
- ***Rest and reset***: Allow time for recovery before launching the next major initiative
- ***Look forward with vision***: Use the momentum to build toward new goals

Leaders who navigate this transition effectively support their teams in avoiding burnout and staying inspired.

Success as a Leadership Legacy

Over time, leaders are remembered not just for what they achieved but for how they achieved it. The highs of success contribute to your leadership legacy, the stories told about you, the emotional impact left on your team, and the standard you helped establish for what is possible.

Leaders who uplift others in their success and shine the spotlight outward build reputational capital and organisational trust. They teach teams that success isn't a zero-sum game but is instead a shared journey.

The Peak Is Real, and It's Worth the Climb

Leadership is a long road. It involves tension, uncertainty, and sacrifice. However, it also features moments that make the entire journey worthwhile. The highs of achievement and team success are not incidental; they are essential. They remind you that your efforts matter, your vision is valid, and your leadership has significance.

Don't overlook or rush past these moments. Allow them to sink in. Share them. Celebrate them. They're not just about performance; they're about people. And they represent one of the most significant rewards of the leadership journey.

Finding Meaning in Leadership Beyond Results

Leadership is often measured by metrics, performance targets, key performance indicators (KPIs), financial returns, and stakeholder satisfaction. While these aspects are essential, they only capture part of the story. Leadership, at its most authentic and enduring, is not just about what you achieve; it is about what you build, nurture, and become. The true essence of leadership goes beyond results. It lies in purpose, relationships, values, growth, and legacy.

The leaders who have the most significant impact are not those who chase outcomes at any cost but those who serve something greater than themselves, who lead with intention, elevate others, and leave their organisations and communities better than they found them. For them, leadership is not just a role; it is a calling.

Why Results Alone Are Not Enough

Results are crucial; they serve as evidence of effectiveness, alignment, and execution. However, results can be superficial if they are disconnected from values, context, or humanity.

A toxic culture can still achieve targets. A demoralised team can still meet deadlines. When leaders focus solely on results, they risk prioritising short-term success over long-term sustainability.

Moreover, leadership based solely on outcomes is susceptible to external fluctuations. A market downturn, a failed product, or changing public sentiment can jeopardise a results-driven identity. Leaders who identify entirely with their achievements can swiftly lose direction when success wavers.

The true meaning of leadership is not circumstantial; it is internal. It stems from aligning with purpose, contributing to others, and maintaining integrity in one's actions. It persists even when external validation fades.

Sources of Meaning in Leadership

Purpose

Purpose is the most bottomless well of meaning. It is the "why" that sustains leaders through pressure, failure, and fatigue. Purpose connects daily work to a larger mission. It might be:

- improving lives through service or innovation
- creating opportunity and equity
- protecting values or advancing a cause
- building something enduring and ethical.

Purpose-driven leaders don't just chase success; they serve something greater than themselves. This perspective turns even mundane tasks into meaningful contributions.

Relationships

At its core, leadership is a human endeavour. The relationships forged along the way, such as mentoring a young professional, navigating challenges with a trusted colleague, and supporting a team through a crisis, are among the richest sources of meaning.

The connection, trust, and influence you cultivate leave a lasting impact. People seldom remember spreadsheets or strategies. They recall how a leader made them feel: heard, respected, and empowered. These moments aren't measured in quarterly reports, but they define legacies.

Integrity

Meaning is found in leading with alignment, where actions are consistent with values. Leaders who operate with integrity experience a profound internal congruence. They understand that they are not compromising who they are for the sake of what they do.

Integrity includes:
- making the hard right decision over the easy wrong
- speaking the truth when it's uncomfortable
- holding others (and oneself) accountable with fairness
- staying true to principles under pressure.

This moral clarity fosters trust, self-respect, and long-term fulfilment. It also assists leaders in navigating complexity without losing their centre.

Growth and Contribution

Leaders also find meaning in personal and collective growth, such as seeing someone they've coached rise to their full potential, learning from a painful mistake and emerging wiser, and building a team culture that outlasts their tenure.

Contribution creates meaning when you leave something behind that continues to benefit others. Whether it's a more inclusive system, a stronger process, or a healthier workplace, leaders who contribute meaningfully live with fewer regrets.

Practices That Deepen Leadership Meaning

Reflect Regularly

Meaning doesn't emerge amid constant movement. Leaders must cultivate space for reflection. Ask:
- What am I learning about myself?
- What impact am I having on others?
- Am I living and leading in alignment with my values?

Journalling, coaching conversations, or quiet walks can help clarify your deeper leadership "why."

Define Success Beyond the Numbers

Develop a personal success statement that encompasses more than just financial or operational outcomes. For instance:
- "Success is when people feel safer and more inspired after working with me."
- "Success is when I make decisions that align with my values, even under pressure."

This shifts the focus from performance to purpose.

Engage in Purposeful Storytelling

Consistently revisit and share stories that embody your mission, stories of lives transformed, obstacles overcome, and values upheld. These narratives ground teams in something larger than daily pressures.

They also remind you why the work matters, especially during hard seasons.

Celebrate the Intangible Wins

Not every win can be charted on a dashboard. Celebrate the quieter victories:
- A conflict resolved respectfully.

- A team member who found their voice.
- A cultural shift that made people feel seen.

These moments are often the most significant and lasting.

Leadership as Service, Not Self

At its most meaningful, leadership transforms into a form of service. It's no longer about control, ego, or advancement; it's about stewardship. About guiding people, protecting values, and leaving a legacy of integrity.

This orientation changes everything. It redefines power not as dominance but as responsibility. It sees influence not as a right but as a duty. And it views success not as applause but as quiet alignment between what you do and who you are.

Service-oriented leaders find calm even in the midst of complexity. Their satisfaction derives not from always being right, but from striving to do what is right. They lead with love, not fear, with generosity, not scarcity, and with grounded conviction, not insecure performance.

The Legacy of Meaningful Leadership

The leaders we remember most aren't necessarily those with the biggest titles or the longest resumes. They are the ones who led with purpose, courage, and heart. Those who treated people with dignity. Those who stood for something. Those who taught others what leadership could be.

A meaningful leadership legacy is established by how individuals grow under your guidance, how values are maintained through your presence, and how purpose is safeguarded during times of pressure.

These legacies can't be bought or forced; they're earned, moment by moment, decision by decision.

Beyond the Bottom Line

Leadership presents a powerful opportunity, not only to influence outcomes but also to impact lives. Beyond mere results lies the real work: the work of character, conscience, and contribution. It is here that meaning is discovered. It is here that joy, courage, and authenticity flourish.

If leadership focuses solely on numbers, it becomes hollow. However, when leadership centres on people, purpose, and principles, it transforms into a force for good, not just within organisations but across the globe.

So let's make results matter. But let's make meaning matter more.

Lead not merely for impact but for significance. Lead not just for success but also for the soul.

Anger and Frustration

Leadership is a profoundly emotional undertaking. While qualities such as composure, empathy, and vision are often praised, other emotions, including anger and frustration, seldom receive genuine attention. These feelings are frequently regarded as inappropriate or unprofessional in leadership roles, especially in public-facing or high-stakes environments. Yet they are authentic, powerful, and when managed wisely, enlightening.

Anger and frustration, when acknowledged and channelled constructively, can act as catalysts for clarity, boundary-setting, and systemic change. When ignored or mismanaged, they have the potential to damage relationships, erode credibility, and foster a toxic leadership environment. Understanding these emotions and learning to navigate through them is crucial for mature, emotionally intelligent leadership.

The Presence of Anger and Frustration

Unmet expectations, perceived injustice, chronic inefficiency, misalignment with values, or a sense of betrayal often incite anger in leadership. Frustration emerges when progress is obstructed, communication fails, or repeated efforts produce no change.

Leaders feel these emotions for reasons such as:
- observing a team that underperforms despite receiving guidance and support
- observing unethical behaviour that remains unaddressed
- confronting ongoing resistance to positive change
- navigating bureaucracy that hinders agility
- being deceived, manipulated, or excluded from important decisions
- observing the organisation or team compromising its core values.

In these moments, anger is not irrational; it's a signal that something significant is being violated, ignored, or jeopardised.

Why Leaders Suppress or Misuse Anger

Many leaders have been socialised to believe that anger has no place in leadership. Consequently, they may:
- suppress it, acting as if everything is alright
- deny it by labelling it as "stress" or "disappointment"
- redirect it, attacking safer or unrelated targets.
- internalise it, which can lead to resentment or burnout.

On the other hand, some leaders express anger destructively through passive aggression, public outbursts, or controlling behaviours. These expressions erode psychological safety and diminish respect.

Neither suppression nor explosion is effective. What leaders need is awareness and agency: the ability to recognise their anger, understand its source, and respond constructively.

The Purpose of Anger

Anger is a natural emotional response to a perceived threat or injustice. In leadership, it often indicates that values are being compromised or that boundaries are being crossed. It can serve several purposes:

- *Clarification*: Anger reveals what matters to you. If you're angry about unethical decisions or poor treatment of staff, it's because you care deeply about integrity and dignity.
- *Motivation*: When channelled, anger creates energy. It pushes leaders out of complacency and into action. It fuels advocacy, reform, and accountability.
- *Protection*: Anger can indicate the need to establish or strengthen boundaries. It enables leaders to assert their voice and safeguard what falls within their sphere of responsibility.

When handled effectively, anger transforms into a leadership asset, a force that cultivates courage rather than destruction.

Strategies for Managing Anger and Frustration Constructively

Recognise the Emotion Without Judgement

Instead of denying or rationalising your anger, acknowledge it. Say to yourself, "I'm angry about how that decision was made." This acknowledgment creates awareness and gives you a moment to pause before reacting.

Explore the Root Cause

Ask, "What value is being violated? What expectation was not met? What past issue might this be triggering?"

Often, the anger is not just about the current situation; it's about something more profound.

Create a Pause Before Responding

Employ breathing techniques, engage in physical movement, or take a break from the situation to reduce physiological intensity. This helps prevent reactive, emotionally charged responses.

Choose the Right Time and Format for Feedback

Anger can lead to meaningful conversations, but these must occur when emotions are regulated and intentions are clear. Choose private and respectful settings to discuss sensitive issues.

Focus on the Message, Not the Emotion

Instead of saying, "You made me angry," say, "I was frustrated by how that decision was made without consultation. Here's why it matters …" This keeps the focus on the impact and accountability.

The Cost of Unaddressed Anger

When anger is ignored or allowed to fester, it manifests in other areas:

- as cynicism or disengagement
- as micromanagement or mistrust
- as passive-aggressive communication
- as burnout or emotional withdrawal.

It also impacts team culture. If a leader consistently bottles up their anger, the team may walk on eggshells, sensing the tension but never grasping its source. On the other hand, if a leader frequently vents or lashes out, they foster fear and instability.

Unprocessed anger is like carrying a heavy backpack; it makes everything more complex and more reactive. Leaders who address anger openly and responsibly lighten their emotional load and lead with greater clarity.

The Role of Self-Compassion and Reflection

Leaders often feel shame about experiencing anger, especially if they consider themselves calm, controlled, or emotionally mature. However, anger is not a failure; it is part of the emotional landscape of leadership. Self-compassion enables leaders to acknowledge: "It's okay that I felt that way. What matters now is how I respond."

Reflection enables leaders to learn from their anger. Consider:

- What does this anger reveal about my values?
- How did I manage it? What worked well? What might I change?
- What changes do I need to make to a system, relationship, or boundary?

This practice turns anger into insight.

Modelling Healthy Emotional Expression

When leaders handle anger transparently and maturely, they demonstrate emotional intelligence. They show their teams that:

- emotions are not shameful
- conflict can be navigated with respect
- assertiveness is not aggression
- boundaries are necessary and healthy.

This cultivates a culture where individuals feel secure to express, challenge, and develop. Emotional maturity at the leadership level establishes the tone for the whole organisation.

Anger as a Leadership Signal, Not a Flaw

Anger and frustration in leadership are not signs of failure; they indicate that you care. They show that something needs attention. They signify that something matters. The question is not whether leaders will feel anger but how they will channel it.

Will it serve as fuel for control or courage? A weapon or a wake-up call?

The best leaders don't pretend to be emotionless. They are emotionally honest but not emotionally volatile. They recognise anger, learn from it, and respond with clarity and purpose. In doing so, they transform a potentially destructive force into a tool for change, accountability, and leadership that is both strong and human.

Productive vs. Destructive Anger

Anger is one of the most misunderstood emotions in leadership. It's often viewed as a liability, a volatile force to be avoided, suppressed, or concealed. And indeed, when mishandled, anger can be deeply destructive, damaging relationships, eroding trust, and undermining leadership credibility. However, when understood and channelled wisely, anger can also be productive. It can signal misalignment, drive necessary change, and sharpen moral clarity.

The key is not to avoid anger but to distinguish between its productive and destructive expressions. Great leaders don't pretend they never feel angry. Instead, they learn to use anger as a source of information, not a weapon, and as fuel for constructive action rather than emotional outbursts.

The Dual Nature of Anger

Anger is a potent emotion. At its core, it serves as a reaction to perceived injustice, threats, disrespect, or breaches of fundamental values. It can offer clarity amid confusion and generate energy when apathy hampers progress. However, it is a fire, and like any fire, it can either warm or destroy, depending on how it is managed.

Productive anger centres on specific issues, their impact, and the potential for improvement.

Destructive anger centres on blame, control, and emotional release.

Understanding this distinction allows leaders to work with anger instead of being controlled by it.

What Productive Anger Looks Like

Productive anger is purposeful, founded on values and outcome-oriented. It emerges from a place of integrity and bravery.

Clarity of Values

Productive anger signals that something important is being compromised, such as fairness, safety, accountability, or respect. It says, "This isn't right, and I care enough to act."

Example: A leader witnessing discriminatory behaviour intervenes firmly, establishes clear expectations, and reinforces an inclusive culture. The emotion is genuine, but so is the clarity of the message.

Purpose-Driven Expression

Rather than venting, productive anger is channelled into dialogue, setting boundaries, or driving change. The leader asks, "What action will make this situation better?"

Example: After repeated delays on a strategic project, a leader expresses frustration in a team meeting, not by blaming individuals but by identifying systemic issues, resetting expectations, and recommitting the group to a timeline.

Controlled Delivery

The emotional intensity is recognised, but the message stays respectful and professional. The leader manages tone, body language, and timing.

Example: A CEO addressing a breach of ethics does so firmly and with emotional weight, but without resorting to personal attacks. They emphasise the seriousness while maintaining their composure.

Constructive Outcomes

Productive anger results in solutions, including changes in processes, more transparent communication, stronger policies, or mended relationships.

What Destructive Anger Looks Like

Destructive anger arises from reactivity, ego, or unresolved personal triggers. While it may seem justified at the time, it often leads to unnecessary harm.

Personal Attacks or Blame

Destructive anger focuses on people rather than problems. It shows itself through criticism, sarcasm, or belittlement.

Example: A leader publicly chastises an employee for a missed deadline without understanding the context or providing support, thereby fostering shame rather than accountability.

Emotional Outbursts

Raised voices, abrupt emails, and passive-aggressive comments indicate anger being dumped rather than directed.

Example: After a failed negotiation, a leader expresses their frustration to the team, creating fear and confusion rather than clarity.

Retaliation or Control

Destructive anger seeks to punish or dominate. It uses power to suppress dissent or reassert authority.

Example: A manager reacts to feedback by sidelining the employee who gave it, rather than reflecting on the substance of the critique.

Repressed Anger

On the opposite extreme, some leaders internalise their anger, letting resentment fester. They become disengaged, cynical, or passive-aggressive, fostering emotional distance and unpredictability.

Consequences of Destructive Anger

Unchecked, destructive anger weakens leadership in several ways:

- *Trust erodes*: People start to fear the leader instead of respecting them.
- *Engagement declines*: Team members hold back ideas or feedback to avoid provoking the leader's temper.
- *Culture suffers*: Emotional volatility or avoidance creates an atmosphere of insecurity.
- *Leader burnout rises*: Suppressed anger saps energy, resulting in fatigue, disconnection, or cynicism.

Leaders who frequently act out of destructive anger may achieve short-term compliance but will likely face long-term disengagement.

Turning Anger into a Leadership Tool

Anger becomes productive when leaders cultivate the skills to recognise, acknowledge, and manage it effectively. This includes:

Emotional Literacy

Learn to identify when you're feeling anger as opposed to disappointment, shame, or fear. The more accurately you can label the emotion, the better you can respond to it.

Self-Regulation

Before responding in anger, take a moment to pause. Use breathing techniques, movement, or time-outs to create a gap between the trigger and your response. This doesn't mean dismissing anger; instead, it involves using it wisely.

Clarify Your Intent

Before conveying anger, consider this:
- What outcome am I after?
- Is this about ego or making an impact?
- Will expressing this emotion benefit the team, the mission, or provide my release?

Own the Emotion, Not Just the Behaviour

It's fine to say, "I'm frustrated by how this played out." When expressed with self-awareness and respect, this form of honesty fosters trust and confidence. It demonstrates healthy emotional expression.

Apologise When Necessary

If your anger spills out destructively, acknowledge it. A genuine apology doesn't diminish authority; it enhances credibility.

Culture and the Normalisation of Anger

In some organisational cultures, destructive anger is tolerated or even rewarded. Aggressive leaders may be viewed as "passionate" or "demanding excellence." However, this normalisation comes at a cost: fear-based compliance, toxic loyalty, and suppressed innovation.

In contrast, cultures that promote emotionally intelligent leadership encourage:
- assertive feedback without demeaning remarks
- expression of frustration without losing control
- resolution of conflict through mutual respect
- psychological safety for every voice, even under pressure.

Leaders shape culture through their emotional expressions. Productive anger becomes a norm when leaders consistently utilise it to protect values and foster positive change.

Fire With Purpose

Anger isn't the enemy of good leadership; it's a signal, a force, a fire. The question is whether that fire burns bridges or lights the way ahead.

Productive anger is a strong tool for accountability, clarity, and courage. It highlights what is essential and mobilises action. In contrast, destructive anger clouds judgement and harms the very relationships that leadership relies on.

To lead with integrity doesn't mean avoiding emotion; it means honouring it without being controlled by it. The most effective leaders learn to channel anger not into control but into constructive leadership that protects people, principles, and progress.

How to Deal with Injustice, Incompetence, or Betrayal

Leadership demands not only skill and strategy but also emotional resilience. At some stage in every leadership journey, you'll encounter moments that test your values, integrity, and resolve when confronted by injustice, incompetence, or betrayal. These moments hurt. They strike at the core of what it means to lead with honour and purpose. They can provoke anger, disbelief, or disillusionment. However, they also present defining choices: to respond with clarity or react with bitterness; to uphold standards or walk away; to protect what matters or safeguard your pride.

Navigating these experiences requires emotional maturity, courage, and a clear understanding of principles. It isn't easy, but it's essential. These moments reveal not just the leader's capabilities but also their character.

Facing Injustice as a Leader

Injustice occurs when fairness, ethics, or moral standards are violated, when people are mistreated, rules are applied unequally, or harm is ignored. Leaders may witness injustice within their organisation or may even experience it themselves.

When You Witness Injustice

Leaders must respond to injustice when they encounter it. Silence can be viewed as complicity. Taking a stand may be uncomfortable, but it signifies integrity and fosters trust.

Actions to consider:
- *Name it clearly*: Don't dilute what occurred. Use precise language; label it as racism, sexism, bullying, or exploitation if that's what it is.
- *Document and escalate*: If necessary, follow formal reporting pathways to ensure accountability and transparency.
- *Support the impacted party*: Reach out, provide protection, and show solidarity.
- *Review policies and culture*: Injustice often indicates systemic flaws. Ask, "What allowed this to occur? What needs to change?"

Leadership in these moments isn't about appearances; it's about moral courage.

When You Experience Injustice

Experiencing injustice, whether through exclusion, discrimination, or unfair treatment, is a painful experience. The temptation is often to retreat, retaliate, or shut down.

To lead through this:
- *Acknowledge the hurt*: Don't minimise what you feel. Injustice cuts deep. Process it with trusted mates or coaches.
- *Decide how to respond*: Not every battle needs to be fought publicly but none should be ignored internally. Choose your path wisely: report, confront, or sometimes, walk away.

- ***Reaffirm your values***: Injustice tries to isolate and disempower. Upholding your values restores dignity and strength.

Dealing with Incompetence

Few things frustrate leaders more than ongoing incompetence, especially when individuals fail to perform despite receiving support or when systemic dysfunction remains unaddressed. Over time, incompetence undermines morale, credibility, and results.

Types of Incompetence
- ***Skill-based***: A person does not possess the necessary ability or training.
- ***Will-based***: The individual is disengaged or reluctant to improve.
- ***Systemic***: The organisation does not address ongoing poor performance.

How to Respond

Diagnose the Root Cause
Ask yourself, "Is this a capacity issue or a motivation issue? Has this person been provided with the resources, clarity, and feedback needed to succeed?"

Be Direct and Compassionate
Avoid sugar-coating. Honest feedback, delivered with care, is a sign of respect. Offer support, but be clear about the consequences that may result.

Set Clear Standards and Timelines
When incompetence is tolerated indefinitely, it sends the message that excellence isn't valued. Be specific about expectations, and follow through on next steps.

Address Systemic Gaps

If incompetence is widespread, look upstream. Are the hiring processes flawed? Is there accountability? Do leaders model the standards they expect others to follow?

Know When to Act Decisively

Chronic incompetence that undermines team wellbeing or mission delivery demands tough decisions, reassignments, exits, or restructures. Delaying only exacerbates the damage.

Responding to Betrayal

Betrayal cuts deeper than errors or disagreements. It represents the breaking of trust when someone you have relied on misleads you, undermines your interests, or acts in their self-interest at your expense. In leadership, betrayal can arise from peers, direct reports, board members, or even mentors.

It evokes powerful emotions: hurt, rage, confusion, grief. It destabilises relationships and undermines your sense of safety.

Steps to Navigate Betrayal

Pause and Reflect

Responding immediately might escalate the situation or cause further harm. Take the time to understand what happened, why it occurred, and how it has affected you emotionally.

Clarify the Facts

What exactly happened? Is this a one-off incident or part of a broader pattern? Betrayal can be personal but your response must be based on reality.

Decide on the Relational Path

You have options:

- ***Repair***: If the person demonstrates genuine remorse and the relationship still holds value, consider rebuilding with boundaries.
- ***Reframe***: Adjust your expectations, set new boundaries, and continue working together while maintaining a healthy distance.
- ***Release***: If trust is irreparably broken, a clean break may be necessary for your peace and the organisation's wellbeing.

Communicate with Maturity

If a conversation is necessary, concentrate on the impact rather than making accusations. Example: "When this happened, it violated the trust I placed in you. Here's what I need going forward."

Protect your Leadership Integrity

Don't resort to retaliation. Safeguard your credibility by leading with grace, even when faced with disappointment. Others are observing how you respond.

Maintaining Your Centre in the Face of Violation

Whether you're facing injustice, incompetence, or betrayal, the risk is not just organisational; it's personal. These experiences can harden you, isolate you, or lead you to question your judgement. That's why self-leadership is so vital.

Re-ground Yourself

- Reflect on your core values, and allow them to guide your response.
- Reflect on your purpose. Why do you lead? What continues to matter?
- Seek support from mentors, peers, and counsellors. Don't bear the emotional burden alone.

Practice Emotional Hygiene
- Write down your feelings instead of bottling them up.
- Get your body moving to let go of tension.
- Participate in renewal rituals, such as meditation, reading, spending time in nature, and engaging in creative outlets.

Lead With Wisdom, Not Woundedness

You can experience hurt and still lead effectively. You can acknowledge pain without allowing it to dictate your decisions. You can establish boundaries without shutting your heart off.

Choosing the Long View

Leadership isn't solely about managing tasks; it's fundamentally about managing meaning. How you interpret injustice, incompetence, or betrayal will influence your growth and legacy. These moments can:
- clarify what you will and won't accept.
- show you who your real allies are
- enhance your boundaries and discernment
- remind you why leadership needs both heart and spine.

If you approach them with intention, these painful moments can turn into pivotal ones, inflection points where you deepen your maturity, resilience, and wisdom.

Leading With Integrity in Imperfect Conditions

You will navigate flawed systems. You will collaborate with people who might let you down. You will encounter situations that seem unfair. These are not indicators of failure; they are signs that you are genuinely leading.

The measure of your leadership isn't about whether these challenges arise but about how you respond to them. Will you become bitter or better? Hardened or wiser? Diminished or deepened?

The best leaders aren't those who've never been betrayed; they are the ones who respond with clarity, courage, and grace. They protect their mission, their people, and their humanity. They lead not despite hardship but through it.

Loneliness and Connection

Leadership is often idealised as a journey of influence, vision, and empowerment. Yet beneath the surface of authority and confidence lies a quieter, more vulnerable reality: loneliness. Leaders are expected to be decisive, resilient, and unwavering in their approach. Still, in the process, they can become emotionally distant from those they lead, isolated by their responsibilities and removed from genuine connection. Paradoxically, while leadership is a profoundly relational role, it can be one of the loneliest paths a person walks.

But loneliness isn't inevitable. When intentionally cultivated, connection can counterbalance the isolation that often comes with leadership. Relationships built on trust, mutual respect, and emotional honesty can provide the grounding a leader needs to thrive, both professionally and personally.

Understanding Leadership Loneliness

Loneliness in leadership isn't just about being alone; it's about feeling isolated and disconnected from others. It's the experience of emotional isolation, a lack of peers to confide in, limited safe spaces to be vulnerable, and few opportunities for genuine connection without the filter of position.

Leaders often feel lonely because:
- They cannot share everything; confidentiality, politics, and emotional risks prevent open sharing.
- They are viewed in different ways. Power dynamics hinder genuine feedback and connection.
- They must make tough decisions independently. While collaboration is essential, ultimate responsibility cannot always be shared.
- They are expected to be strong; admitting emotional needs or uncertainty can feel like a risk to one's credibility.

This can lead to a disconnect between a leader's public persona and their private reality, leaving them surrounded by people yet emotionally solitary.

The Costs of Loneliness

Loneliness is not only unpleasant but also dangerous. When left unaddressed, it can lead to:
- ***Distorted thinking***: Isolated leaders may become excessively self-reliant, wary, or hesitant to take risks.
- ***Increase stress***: Unshared emotional burdens lead to burnout.
- ***Reduce empathy***: Disconnection may dull emotional sensitivity, resulting in a colder, more transactional leadership style.
- ***Undermine decision-making***: Without trusted confidants, leaders may struggle to challenge their assumptions or biases.

Most importantly, chronic loneliness can strip leadership of its humanity, turning a relational role into an existential burden.

The Power of Connection

While loneliness might feel inevitable, it isn't inescapable. Leaders who recognise the significance of connection and carve out time and space for it lead more authentically, sustainably, and effectively.

Connection isn't about being liked or popular.
- Being known means having someone who understands the burden you bear.
- Being trusted means knowing you can express yourself freely without the fear of judgement.
- Being supported means feeling supported both emotionally and intellectually.

These connections can originate from within the organisation or from outside it.

Building Meaningful Connections as a Leader

Develop Trusted Peer Relationships

Every leader needs a circle of peers, not subordinates or competitors, who understand the unique challenges of leadership. Whether through formal networks or casual friendships, these relationships are essential.

Look for:
- fellow executives from other sectors
- professional associations
- leadership forums and mastermind groups.

Set aside time for regular informal chats. Talk not just about strategy but also emotion, meaning, and purpose.

Find a Mentor or Coach

A mentor or coach offers a safe, non-judgemental environment for reflection, venting, exploration, and growth. They provide both support and accountability. Regular conversations with a wise guide can serve as an anchor in times of stress or uncertainty.

Be Vulnerable (Appropriately) With Your Team
Connecting with your team doesn't mean oversharing; it means being human. Admit when you don't have all the answers, acknowledge shared challenges, and express gratitude. Authenticity fosters connection.

Leaders who exemplify appropriate vulnerability foster cultures of trust and psychological safety.

Invest in Personal Relationships
Don't let your role take over your life. Set aside time for those who remind you of who you are beyond your title, such as family, friends, mentors, and your community. These relationships recharge your emotional energy.

Reflect and Reconnect With Yourself
At times, the most profound loneliness arises from a disconnection from oneself. Engaging in activities such as journalling, meditation, spending time in nature, or participating in creative pursuits can help restore internal alignment. A connected leader is someone who leads not only others but also themselves.

Overcoming the Shame of Loneliness
One reason many leaders suffer in silence is that loneliness feels shameful. Leaders are meant to be "above" such feelings, resilient, emotionally self-sufficient, and always in control.

But the truth is, loneliness isn't a weakness; it's a signal. A signal that you are human, that you need a connection, and that your emotional world matters.

Talking openly about loneliness doesn't diminish your credibility; it makes you relatable. It allows others to be honest, too. It helps dismantle the myth of the invulnerable leader.

Reframing Connection as a Leadership Strength

Rather than undermining leadership, emotional connection actually enhances it. Leaders who are connected:
- pay closer attention
- make more thoughtful decisions
- foster more committed teams
- inspire confidence
- lead with compassion.

Connection isn't a distraction from performance; it's the foundation of it. It builds the emotional infrastructure for sustainable leadership.

When Connection is Not Possible

There will be seasons when connection feels elusive, when politics, role changes, or personal transitions create a sense of distance. During those times:
- Ground yourself in your values.
- Establish healthy boundaries.
- Stay connected to your purpose.
- Look for even the smallest moments of human connection; one honest conversation can help re-ground you.

Remember: loneliness is a state, not a sentence. It can be changed, even if slowly.

Leading Together, Not Alone

Leadership may be lonely, but it shouldn't be isolating. Connection is not a luxury for leaders; it's a lifeline. It humanises the role, protects the soul, and sustains the journey. No leader thrives in a vacuum. No vision is realised in isolation.

So reach out. Build your circle. Open your heart. Allow yourself to be supported.

Leadership isn't about standing above others; it's about standing alongside them. Connection isn't just what makes leadership bearable; it's what makes it worthwhile.

The Isolation of Leadership

Leadership, for all its purpose and power, carries an emotional paradox: the higher you rise, the more isolated you may feel. While surrounded by people, decisions, and noise, leaders often operate in an emotional vacuum, disconnected from candid feedback, peer-level connection, and opportunities to express vulnerability. This isn't just a psychological challenge; it's a strategic risk. When unaddressed, isolation can distort judgement, narrow perspective, and undermine the very foundation of effective leadership.

Understanding the nature of leadership isolation and developing strategies to address it is crucial for anyone in a significant position of responsibility. It requires humility, self-awareness, and a deliberate effort to stay connected, grounded, and relationally aware.

The Forms of Leadership Isolation

Leadership isolation doesn't occur all at once. It creeps in through subtle dynamics, structural realities, and cultural expectations. It manifests in three key ways:

1. Positional Isolation

Leadership establishes a gap between the leader and the team, bridging authority and approachability. Power distances frequently lead to filtered information, cautious conversations, and reluctance to challenge the leader's views.

Leaders might observe:
- people expressing what they believe the leader wishes to hear
- a shortage of genuine upward feedback
- limited interaction with peers.

This separation may result in a disconnection from reality, the formation of echo chambers, and decisions made in isolation.

2. Emotional Isolation

Leaders are expected to be composed, rational, and confident, even in times of crisis. Consequently, they often feel unable to express doubt, fatigue, or frustration.

This creates an emotional bottleneck. Leaders suppress their feelings to "stay strong," but over time, this results in:
- numbness or emotional exhaustion
- repressed anger or anxiety
- difficulty empathising with others.

Leadership turns into an emotional performance rather than a genuine experience.

3. Relational Isolation

Leaders often have fewer genuine peers within their organisation. Colleagues are typically subordinates, stakeholders, or political actors. As trust becomes more selective, relational intimacy may decrease.

This can lead to:
- a diminishing group of trusted friends

- constant vigilance and caution
- loss of social spontaneity.

Eventually, the leader's world may shrink, reinforcing feelings of "no one understands what I'm going through."

Causes of Leadership Isolation

Several forces contribute to this phenomenon:
- ***Organisational hierarchy***: The authority structure inherently restricts openness and equality in relationships.
- ***Expectation of invulnerability***: Leaders are often expected to provide emotional support to others, even when they're feeling lost themselves.
- ***Fear of misinterpretation***: Vulnerability can be weaponised in certain cultures; a candid moment can be reframed as a sign of weakness.
- ***Role overload***: Time pressures and decision fatigue squeeze out opportunities for reflection and connection.
- ***Self-Protection***: Following betrayal or organisational politics, leaders might withdraw as a protective measure.

Consequences of Isolation

If left unaddressed, leadership isolation significantly affects the leader, the team, and the organisation.

Poor Decision-Making

Without honest input and diverse perspectives, leaders may make flawed or biased decisions. Blind spots increase in isolation.

Decreased Innovation

Isolation stifles creativity, as leaders who feel disconnected or out of touch tend to exhibit a decline in risk-taking and innovative thinking.

Emotional Exhaustion

The psychological impact of bearing unshared burdens leads to stress, fatigue, and ultimately, burnout.

Erosion of Culture

An isolated leader creates a ripple effect: teams grow cautious, communication becomes politicised, and authenticity vanishes.

Damaged Reputation

When leaders are aloof or reactive, it undermines trust. Team members might disengage or seek leadership elsewhere.

Strategies to Overcome Leadership Isolation

Awareness is the first antidote to isolation. Once recognised, leaders can begin taking deliberate steps to reconnect with themselves, their teams, and trusted peers.

Build a Peer Network

Engage with other leaders beyond your organisation. Leadership forums, mastermind groups, or informal peer circles provide a space for shared experiences, open conversations, and mutual support.

Foster an Inner Circle of Trust

Even in hierarchical settings, identify a few trusted individuals, like mentors, advisors, or direct reports, who can provide honest feedback. Foster psychological safety in these relationships.

Work With a Coach or Mentor

A leadership coach or mentor offers structured reflection, challenges, and emotional support. They foster a safe environment for discussing dilemmas, failures, and uncertainties.

Model Vulnerability Wisely

Share moments of uncertainty or personal insight when it's appropriate. Let your team see your humanity. When done with care, this builds a connection without compromising authority.

Create Space for Reflection

Set aside time in your schedule for solitude that heals rather than isolates. Journal, meditate, walk, or think away from the noise. Solitude can be regenerative if it's intentional.

Listen Without Filtering

Actively seek input, and allow others to express differing opinions. Reward honesty. Avoid surrounding yourself with yes-men. The best leaders cultivate environments where dissent is safe and encouraged.

Reframing the Leadership Role

Sometimes, isolation stems from a flawed mental model of leadership, which views it as the lone genius, the hero, or the infallible expert. This archetype is both unrealistic and harmful.

Instead, leaders can adopt a new mindset:
- Leadership is about relationships, not just titles.
- Power is something to be shared, not hoarded.
- Courage encompasses vulnerability.
- Success encompasses wellbeing.

This reframing fosters a more sustainable and humane form of leadership, in which connection and collaboration are seen not as risks but as essential requirements.

When Isolation is Chronic or Cultural

If a leader operates in a culture that rewards secrecy, discourages feedback, or punishes vulnerability, systemic isolation can occur. In these cases:

- Identify allies who can help shift the culture.
- Identify the issue (carefully and strategically).
- Focus on organisational health, not just performance. Consider if the environment still aligns with your leadership values.

At times, remaining in such a context may compromise your integrity. Opting to leave can be a form of leadership by itself.

Alone at the Top? Only If You Let It Be

The phrase "it's lonely at the top" has endured because it contains a truth. Leadership brings responsibilities that are often invisible, burdens that cannot always be shared. However, loneliness is not the same as necessary solitude, and isolation is not a prerequisite for influence.

Leadership doesn't have to be a lonely climb. You can invite others into your thinking. You can create feedback loops. You can develop peer communities. You can ask for assistance.

Ultimately, the most impactful leaders are not those who stand above; they are the ones who remain among their peers. They are connected, curious, and brave enough to let others see the whole human behind the title.

Building Trusted Relationships and Psychological Safety

Leadership is not only about setting strategy or making decisions; it's about cultivating an environment where people can thrive and reach their full potential. At the heart of this is trust. Without trust, even the most brilliant strategies are doomed to fail. Without psychological safety, teams withhold their best thinking. In today's complex and high-pressure workplaces, leaders must create conditions where people feel safe to speak up, take risks, admit mistakes, and be themselves. This is not a "soft" skill; it is a core leadership competency.

Building trusted relationships and fostering psychological safety necessitates intention, consistency, and emotional intelligence. It involves how leaders present themselves each day, how they communicate, listen, challenge, support, and respond when things go awry. When executed effectively, it transforms teams from cautious and compliant to bold and collaborative.

Why Trust and Psychological Safety Matter

In high-trust, psychologically safe environments:

- People share their ideas without fear of embarrassment or punishment.
- Conflict is handled constructively, not avoided or escalated.
- Mistakes should be acknowledged and learned from, not concealed.
- Innovation and collaboration thrive.
- Performance improves not due to pressure but because of belief and buy-in.

Conversely, in low-trust environments:
- Employees often manage up instead of being truthful.
- Feedback is withheld.
- Groupthink dominates.
- Talented individuals may disengage or leave.

A leader's ability to foster trust and safety isn't just a "nice to have"; it's a competitive advantage and a cultural necessity.

Understanding Psychological Safety

Psychological safety, a term popularised by Harvard professor Amy Edmondson[5], refers to the shared belief that it is safe to take interpersonal risks within a team. It's not merely about feeling comfortable all the time; it's about being respected and secure, even when conversations become complicated.

A psychologically safe culture means you can:
- admit you don't know something
- ask for help without looking weak
- challenge authority without retribution
- fail, learn, and try again without being humiliated.

---

5. https://hbr.org/podcast/2019/01/creating-psychological-safety-in-the-workplace

This is particularly vital in leadership settings that demand agility, creativity, and a strong sense of accountability.

The Foundation: Trust

Trust forms the essential foundation of psychological safety. Without it, individuals won't engage honestly or take risks. Trust is built on three key elements:

1. **Competence**: "I trust that you can do the job well."
2. **Character**: "I trust that you will act ethically and fairly."
3. **Care**: "I trust that you genuinely have my interests at heart."

When trust is strong across all three dimensions, people are more engaged. If any dimension is lacking, they withdraw.

How Leaders Build Trusted Relationships

Consistency Over Time

Trust isn't built through grand gestures; consistent behaviours shape it. Do what you say you'll do. Be reliable. Make time for others, even when it's inconvenient.

Small, consistent signals of reliability create a climate of safety.

Communicate With Transparency

Be honest about what you know, what you don't know, and what actions you're taking. Avoid spin. Acknowledge complexity. Encourage dialogue.

Transparency demonstrates respect and fosters credibility.

Show Vulnerability

Vulnerability fosters connection. When leaders acknowledge mistakes, seek feedback, or share challenges (appropriately), they humanise themselves. This decreases the emotional barrier for others to follow suit.

Vulnerability isn't a weakness; it's a leadership strength when exercised with intention.

Practice Active Listening

Listening is the currency of trust. Avoid interrupting, dismissing, or rushing to problem-solve. Allow the other person to be heard completely before responding.

Pose follow-up questions. Echo what you've heard. Show that you appreciate people for their honesty, even when it's uncomfortable.

Provide Candid, Constructive Feedback

Trust doesn't mean avoiding hard truths; it means delivering them with care and clarity. Frame feedback around growth, not blame. Be specific. Offer support. Follow up.

People trust leaders who are willing to speak the truth and support them in their personal and professional growth.

Protect Others' Dignity

When people fail, how you respond is essential. Humiliation destroys trust, while accountability paired with compassion builds it.

Correct in private, not publicly. Discuss behaviour rather than identity, and differentiate between performance and worth.

Creating Psychological Safety at the Team Level

Psychological safety isn't established in isolation; it needs to be fostered throughout the whole team. Here's how leaders can cultivate it.

Set Norms Around Respectful Challenge

Clarify that disagreement is both welcome and anticipated. Demonstrate how to question ideas without attacking the individuals who hold them. Emphasise that constructive dissent strengthens the team.

Acknowledge Your Fallibility

Regularly say things like:
- "I might be wrong; what do you think?"
- "What am I missing?"
- "I'd love your perspective on this."

This shifts the culture from defensiveness to curiosity.

Respond Supportively to Risk-Taking

When someone speaks up, takes a risk, or admits a mistake, reward them. Say thank you. Recognise the courage. Please encourage others to build upon it.

What gets recognised gets repeated.

Address Incivility and Exclusion Immediately

Nothing undermines psychological safety faster than tolerating toxic behaviour. If someone belittles, interrupts, or marginalises others, step in. Establish the tone. Safeguard the environment.

Safety must be maintained.

Barriers to Building Trust and Safety

Even well-intentioned leaders might find it challenging to build trust if they:
- avoid conflict or sugar-coat reality
- overreact to mistakes
- micromanage out of fear

- lack self-awareness about their impact
- allow high performers to act with impunity.

Being aware of these pitfalls is the first step to changing behaviour. Trust is fragile, yet it is also resilient when fostered with consistency and care.

Leading Through Breaches of Trust

Trust will be broken at times by leaders or by others. What matters most is how you respond.
- Acknowledge the breach openly.
- Apologise sincerely, and take responsibility.
- Explain the changes or boundaries that will follow.
- Invite feedback, and commit to repair.

Restoring trust takes time, but it is achievable when approached with humility and a commitment to follow through.

Trust and Safety as Leadership Multipliers

Ultimately, trust and psychological safety aren't just about making people feel good; they're about ensuring individuals feel safe enough to do their best work.

They allow teams to take risks, express their thoughts, and develop together. They lessen fear and enhance belonging. Moreover, they make leadership sustainable; it's not a lonely burden but a shared journey.

Trusted leaders foster loyal teams. Safe environments encourage innovation. In a world marked by volatility and complexity, these qualities are not optional; they are essential.

So lead with consistency. Speak with clarity. Listen with care. Protect what matters. And remember: the strongest teams aren't those that avoid difficulty; they are the ones where people feel safe enough to face it together.

Hope and Vision

In times of change, uncertainty, or crisis, leaders are often called upon for guidance. Yet, beyond technical solutions or tactical plans, there is something deeper that people seek: hope. They want to believe that the future can be better and that someone has the vision and resolve to lead them there. Hope, paired with vision, is one of the most potent emotional tools a leader can wield.

Leadership rooted in hope isn't mere unquestioning optimism or wishful thinking. It's the deliberate fostering of belief in a better tomorrow, anchored in values, purpose, and direction. Vision provides people with something to strive for. Hope offers them the strength to persevere.

Understanding Hope as a Leadership Force

Hope is an emotion focused on the future that encompasses:
- a belief that improvement is possible
- a sense of agency (that we can influence outcomes)
- a path forward, even if difficult.

It contrasts with naive positivity. Hope recognises hardship while maintaining faith in progress. It is grounded in resilience and a sense of meaning.

Leaders who instil hope:
- inspire action in the face of adversity
- reframe obstacles as challenges, not dead ends
- sustain morale over long journeys
- anchor people emotionally when circumstances are unstable.

Hope isn't soft; it's strategic. It's what drives people forward when logic suggests giving up.

The Role of Vision

Vision is the articulation of a compelling future state, an image of what could be. It provides direction for energy, coherence for strategy, and purpose for effort. However, vision alone is insufficient. To truly matter, it must be shared and felt.

A powerful leadership vision has five qualities:

1. ***Clarity***: It's clear and concrete enough to visualise.
2. ***Credibility***: It's believable and grounded in reality.
3. ***Ambition***: It motivates individuals to exceed the status quo.
4. ***Relevance***: It resonates with people's values and aspirations.
5. ***Emotion***: It inspires pride, purpose, and motivation.

Without a vision, teams drift. Without hope, they stall. Leadership weaves both into a force that moves forward.

How Leaders Cultivate Hope Through Vision

Tell a Compelling Story

Facts alone don't generate hope; stories do. Leaders must portray the future not just as a series of goals but as a narrative: who we are, where we're headed, and why it matters.

A good vision story encompasses hardship, agency, and triumph.

Example: "We're not just adapting to change; we're shaping the future of this industry together."

Honour the Past, But Lead to the Future

Hope isn't denial of what's been lost; it's the belief that something meaningful still lies ahead. Leaders who recognise the challenges while looking forward gain credibility.

Example: "We've been through tough seasons before, and each time, we've emerged stronger. This moment is no different."

Break It Down into Milestones

Hope can feel abstract. Tangible milestones make it real. Leaders translate their vision into steps, including short-term, mid-term, and long-term progress indicators that people can rally behind.

Example: "Within 6 months, we'll launch the new platform. Within 12, we'll double our reach. And within 2 years, we'll redefine how our community engages with us."

Embody the Vision

People look to leaders not just to cast the vision but to embody it. Leaders who align their behaviour with their beliefs demonstrate integrity and foster hope through action.

Example: A leader advocating for innovation must also be willing to take risks. A leader championing wellbeing must model balance.

Hope During Crisis and Change

In times of disruption, whether economic, political, organisational, or existential, hope becomes urgent. During these periods, leaders must:
- be transparent about what is known and unknown
- allow room for grief or frustration
- maintain a consistent emotional tone
- discuss not only problems but also possibilities.

Hope during a crisis isn't false reassurance; it's a vital lifeline. It's the belief that meaning and momentum can still be discovered. It's the reminder: this is not the end of the story.

The Emotional Mechanics of Hope

Hope has physiological and psychological benefits.
- It reduces stress by shifting focus to possibilities.
- It activates the motivation centres in the brain.
- It enhances perseverance and creativity.
- It counteracts emotional fatigue.

Leaders who consciously generate hope energise their teams. They shift the group's focus from threats to opportunities, without denying the existence of risks.

Barriers to Hope and Vision

Leaders may struggle to instil hope when they:
- feel disillusioned or burnt out
- communicate uncertainty without confidence
- over-focus on metrics without meaning
- isolate themselves from the team's emotional reality.

The antidote is to reconnect with purpose. When leaders rediscover what matters most and why the mission exists, they can start to re-anchor hope in the service of something larger than themselves.

Hope as a Collective Asset

Hope is not something a leader imposes; it is something they cultivate. It grows when:
- people feel heard and included
- success is shared and celebrated
- teams are reminded of their progress
- culture reflects shared values and vision.

Leaders shape the emotional climate of their organisations. A hopeful climate fosters engagement, loyalty, innovation, and wellbeing.

Vision is the Compass, Hope is the Fuel

Leadership is not just about getting things done; it's about guiding people towards something worthwhile. Hope and vision are what make that journey sustainable. They give people meaning, motivation, and emotional resilience.

In every leadership season, whether it's one of growth, survival, or reinvention. Hope and vision are not luxuries. They are non-negotiable. Without them, leadership becomes mechanical. With them, it becomes transformational.

So speak the vision. Nurture the hope. Lead with both heart and foresight. The future depends on it.

The Role of Optimism in Inspiring Others

Leadership is ultimately about influence, not just over actions but also over mindset, mood, and meaning. Among the most potent emotional influences a leader can wield is optimism. Optimism fuels hope, inspires performance, and helps people believe in what is possible, even in the face of complexity or adversity.

Optimism is not naive positivity. It is not blind to risk or difficulty. Instead, it is the belief that through effort, collaboration, and creativity, better outcomes can be achieved. Optimism energises. It creates momentum. It draws people in.

Leaders who lead with optimism don't just imagine a better future; they make others want to help build it.

What Is Optimism in Leadership?

Optimism in leadership is a mindset and communication style that:

- focuses on potential, not just problems
- highlights opportunity in the face of a challenge
- reinforces belief in the team's ability to overcome
- anchors actions in purpose and possibility.

It is not the denial of difficulty but the refusal to be defined or limited by it.

Optimistic leaders bring a "yes, and ..." energy to conversations. They recognise what is wrong and suggest what is possible. They model resilience without pretending that everything is fine.

Why Optimism Matters

In a rapidly changing, high-pressure environment, individuals naturally gravitate towards leaders who help them feel safe, motivated, and hopeful. Optimism plays a crucial role in achieving this by:

Inspiring Action

People are more inclined to act when they believe success is achievable. Optimism lessens the fear of failure and boosts the willingness to participate.

Building Confidence

Optimism boosts self-efficacy, the belief that we can influence outcomes. Leaders who express confidence in their teams lift morale and performance.

Enhancing Adaptability

Optimistic teams demonstrate greater resilience. They perceive change as a challenge to be managed, rather than a threat to be shunned.

Improving Culture

An optimistic tone from leadership establishes the emotional rhythm of the organisation, fostering a positive, open, and energised culture.

The Neuroscience of Optimism

Optimism activates areas of the brain associated with motivation and problem-solving. It boosts dopamine levels, which are associated with focus, creativity, and reward-driven behaviour.

Leaders who effectively model optimism assist in shifting their team's mindset from a perspective of threat to one of possibility, which in turn:
- lowers stress
- improves collaboration
- increases innovation.

This shift is crucial during periods of uncertainty, when the brain often defaults to fear and defensiveness.

How Leaders Express Optimism

Through Language

Optimistic leaders use language that uplifts, includes, and activates. They speak of challenges rather than crises, next steps instead of dead ends, and lessons instead of losses.

Examples:
- We have a challenging road ahead, but I trust this team's capability to steer through it.
- We've navigated more challenging times and come out stronger. Let's do it again.

Through Framing

Optimism is influenced by how leaders frame events. Rather than concentrating solely on what went wrong, they emphasise what can be learned or what progress has been made.

Example:
- Yes, we missed the target, but we've closed the gap significantly, and that tells me we're on the right track.

Through Action

Optimism is reinforced by behaviour. Leaders who take visible, values-aligned steps build credibility. They don't just talk about possibilities; they create them.

Example:
- Launching a pilot project, even amid budget cuts, to explore a bold idea demonstrates faith in the future.

Through Recognition

Celebrating wins, no matter how small, helps keep the energy high. Optimistic leaders acknowledge effort, learning, creativity, and perseverance.

Example:
- "That solution was innovative. Even though it didn't work as planned, the thinking behind it propels us forward."

Optimism vs. Toxic Positivity

It's crucial to distinguish between optimism and toxic positivity. Toxic positivity denies or downplays difficulties in an attempt to maintain a falsely cheerful atmosphere. It:

- dismisses emotions
- discourages open dialogue
- suppresses opposition.

In contrast, genuine optimism recognises pain or challenge and provides a meaningful path forward.

Healthy optimism suggests: "I see the problem. I believe in us. Let's work towards a solution together."

Building a Culture of Optimism

Optimism must extend beyond the individual leader to influence team dynamics and culture. To foster an optimistic environment:

- ***Encourage possibility thinking***: Ask, "What could we try?" instead of, "Why won't this work?"
- ***Balance realism with belief***: Share risks openly, but also explain what's still within our control.
- ***Implement positive rituals***: Begin meetings by celebrating successes and achievements. Conclude projects by reflecting on both the progress and the purpose.
- ***Hire and promote optimistic communicators***: Individuals who inspire, energise, and collaboratively solve problems.

Culture follows leadership. The way a leader presents themselves emotionally sets the tone for what becomes normal in the team.

When Optimism Is Hard to Maintain

Even the most visionary leaders experience periods of fatigue or uncertainty. When that occurs:

- take time to reconnect with purpose
- lean on mentors or peers to restore perspective
- acknowledge your emotional state honestly
- share your humanity without burdening others with your despair.

Sustainable optimism isn't about suppressing pain; it's about processing it with intention and recommitting to what truly matters.

Examples of Optimistic Leadership

- **Jacinda Ardern,** the former Prime Minister of New Zealand, blended empathy with decisive optimism, particularly during crises such as COVID-19 and the Christchurch shootings.
- **Barack Obama** built a political movement around the phrase "Yes, we can," which reflects a belief in collective agency and progress.
- **Satya Nadella,** CEO of Microsoft, transformed the company culture by shifting from a competitive, know-it-all mindset to one characterised by curiosity and growth, driven by optimistic possibility.

These leaders demonstrate that optimism, when paired with competence and compassion, becomes a catalytic force.

Optimism as a Strategic Asset

Optimism isn't just a temperament; it's a leadership tool. When used wisely, it inspires others, fuels resilience, and transforms vision into momentum. It creates a magnetic force that draws people towards shared possibilities.

The role of optimism in leadership is not to pretend that everything is always okay. It is to remind people that they can improve situations. That their work is significant. That the future is not predetermined, and through effort, creativity, and belief, change is achievable.

Optimistic leaders don't just help teams survive; they help them soar.

Emotional Energy in Strategic Foresight

Strategic foresight, the ability to anticipate, shape, and prepare for future possibilities, is often regarded as an intellectual exercise. It involves scanning trends, analysing data, building scenarios, and identifying emerging opportunities or threats. However, what is frequently overlooked is the emotional dimension of foresight. At the core of a leader's ability to think long-term, inspire belief in a better future, and make bold decisions amid uncertainty lies a crucial fuel: emotional energy.

Strategic thinking without emotional energy becomes cold, abstract, and disconnected from people. Emotional energy lacking strategic direction can become scattered or reactive. Outstanding leadership fuses the two, combining the clarity of foresight with the vitality of feeling to advance people and systems.

What Is Emotional Energy in Leadership?

Emotional energy is the inner force that drives engagement, motivation, and connection. It encompasses:

- passion for the mission
- optimism about the future
- resilience in the face of challenge
- presence in moments that matter.

In strategic contexts, emotional energy is what enables leaders to:

- care deeply about what lies ahead
- maintain focus and trust over extended periods of tim.
- express possibilities in ways that encourage action
- keep commitment strong, even when the journey is unclear or taking longer than expected.

Without emotional energy, foresight remains theoretical. With it, foresight becomes transformational.

Why Emotional Energy Matters in Strategic Foresight

It Sustains Vision Over Time

Strategic change requires time. Emotional energy helps leaders and teams stay focused and inspired throughout long journeys. It serves as the antidote to cynicism, drift, and fatigue.

It Fuels Creativity and Scenario Thinking

Emotionally energised leaders are more open to divergent thinking. They're curious, imaginative, and unafraid to challenge assumptions, key ingredients for developing robust, dynamic strategies.

It Builds Commitment to Long-Term Goals

Foresight often necessitates taking action today for benefits that may not emerge for years. Emotional energy cultivates the conviction and patience required to invest in future returns.

It Enhances Communication and Buy-In

Strategic plans only succeed if people believe in them. Emotional energy empowers leaders to craft compelling stories, connect on a personal level, and drive momentum.

The Emotional Demands of Strategic Thinking

Thinking long-term is inherently challenging. It involves grappling with:

- *Ambiguity*: The future is uncertain, and data is imperfect.
- *Disruption*: Foresight often reveals uncomfortable truths about the need for change.
- *Dissonance*: Strategic direction may challenge current norms or power structures.
- *Delayed gratification*: The reward for long-term investment is often far in the future.

These challenges can be exhausting. Leaders need to tap into emotional energy to stay steady, clear, and courageous when faced with complexity.

Sources of Emotional Energy in Strategic Leadership

Purpose and Meaning

Leaders who possess a strong sense of purpose derive significant emotional energy from their work. When the "why" is clear and personal, it becomes easier to navigate uncertainty.

Example: A CEO leading digital transformation because they believe it will make the company more sustainable and future-fit, not just more profitable.

Connection and Community

Relationships matter. Leaders who feel supported and connected to a broader mission gain emotional resilience. Conversation, collaboration, and shared vision all replenish energy.

Optimism and Future Orientation

Optimism fuels persistence. Leaders who believe that the future can be shaped, rather than just endured, draw energy from envisioning and influencing what's next.

Reflection and Recovery

Energy needs to be managed. Leaders who make time for solitude, reflection, or renewal tend to maintain their emotional strength over time. Strategic insight is cultivated in stillness as much as in analysis.

Balancing Rational Strategy with Emotional Energy

Strategic foresight requires rigour. However, rigour without emotional resonance results in sterile strategies that no one claims ownership of. The most effective leaders balance logic and emotion.

- *Logic asks*: What trends are emerging? What scenarios seem likely?
- *Feeling asks*: What future do we envision? What matters to us? What's on the line?

This emotional dimension is not a distraction; it's a guide. It helps leaders prioritise what matters most. It fuels a sense of urgency for change. It anchors strategy in human purpose.

Communicating Strategy With Emotional Energy

Strategic foresight only becomes meaningful when it resonates with others. Emotionally energised communication brings foresight to life.
- Use stories to illustrate possibilities.
- Share your hopes and fears honestly.
- Speak to both the head and the heart.
- Invite others to co-create the future.

When a strategy is communicated with emotional energy, it transforms into something people want to engage with, rather than just something they're instructed to implement.

Emotional Fatigue: A Foresight Risk

Just as energy fuels foresight, its absence diminishes it. Leaders may experience:
- ***Strategic fatigue:*** Exhaustion from constant adaptation or planning
- ***Emotional depletion:*** Burnout, particularly after extended periods of crisis or transformation
- ***Cynicism:*** A loss of belief in the possibility of change.

Recognising and addressing these states is essential. Foresight cannot be sustained from a place of emotional emptiness. Leaders must regularly learn to restore their energy.

Regenerating Emotional Energy

To maintain emotional energy for strategic work.
- Protect time for future-focused thinking.
- Celebrate progress, not just completion.
- Ground each planning cycle in purpose.

- Balance urgency with empathy.
- Invest in personal renewal.

Strategic foresight is not a sprint; it's a long climb. Leaders must pace themselves, bring others along, and rest when necessary.

Embodying the Future You Envision

The most powerful leaders don't merely predict the future; they embody it—their emotional energy conveys belief, clarity, and commitment.

They show up as:
- **hopeful**, not just informed
- **purposeful**, not just reactive
- **curious**, not just confident.

This presence fosters trust, creates alignment, and inspires others to lead with a future-focused mindset.

Energised Foresight Is Human-Centred Foresight

At its best, strategic foresight isn't a cold process of prediction. It's a profoundly human act of imagining, planning, and committing to a future that truly matters. This act demands energy, not only cognitive but also emotional.

Emotion fuels vision. Emotion drives belief. Emotion sustains the long-term effort needed to turn foresight into reality.

So invest in your emotional energy. Protect your purpose. Stay curious. Replenish often. And remember, it's not just what you see in the future that matters; it's how you feel about it and how that feeling moves others to act.

Personal Reflection: The Emotional Spectrum

There was a chapter in my life that tested every part of me. Not just my strategic thinking or decision-making ability but my emotional endurance.

I had taken on a new role, which required me to make adjustments to the organisation's culture. Some staff were toxic and causing good staff to leave. Additionally, the financial situation wasn't the best. Significant changes would have to be made to get the company back on track.

Everything felt uncertain. The structure was shifting, teams were unsettled, and eyes were on me to bring clarity. Beneath the surface, I was quietly carrying fear: fear of getting it wrong, fear of losing people's trust, and fear that maybe I wasn't the right leader for this moment.

I remember sitting in my office late one night, papers scattered across my desk, heart heavy, unsure what to do next. That's when the doubt crept in. Not loud or dramatic. Just the quiet erosion of confidence. I questioned my judgement, my timing, even my value. But deep down, I knew what I believed in: fairness, transparency, and caring for people. The conviction gave me just enough confidence to take the next step.

In the weeks that followed, I felt everything. Anger at the resistance, the games, the unnecessary pain caused by a few who put ego before the team. Loneliness in the moments when, despite a full calendar and constant noise, the burden of leadership felt entirely mine. But I also found joy. Unexpected joy, in fact, in the resilience of people who showed up every day with grace, in the small wins, in the shared laughter during hard days.

And most of all, I found hope. Not blind optimism but the grounded belief that if we kept showing up, honestly, humanly, and with integrity, things would get better. And they did.

That chapter in my life didn't break me. It refined me. It reminded me that leadership isn't about mastering emotions; it's about walking with them. All of them. Fear and courage. Doubt and resolve. Frustration and fulfilment. Loneliness and connection. And always, always hope.

That's what makes leadership deeply human and, ultimately, worth it.

PART THREE

Emotional Mastery in Action

Leading Through Crisis

Crisis reveals the essence of leadership. It strips away the comfortable, the routine, and the predictable, exposing character, clarity, and conviction. When uncertainty dominates and stakes are high, people look to leaders not just for answers but for guidance and reassurance. In moments of disruption, whether due to economic shock, natural disaster, organisational failure, or societal upheaval, leadership is not just about managing logistics; it's about managing emotion, expectation, and meaning.

Leading through crisis demands decisiveness, empathy, and steadiness. But more than anything, it requires the courage to show up, not as a perfect authority figure but as a human capable of making sense, providing direction, and holding the space for others.

Understanding the Nature of Crisis

A crisis is not just a bad day. It is a profound interruption of standard systems, marked by:

- *Urgency*: Decisions must be made quickly, often with incomplete information.

- **Complexity**: No clear solutions, many moving parts.
- **High stakes**: Consequences are real, often involving safety, stability, or survival.
- **Emotional volatility**: Fear, anger, grief, and confusion are widespread.

In these conditions, traditional leadership tools often fall short. What people need is not just competence but calm. Not just authority but assurance.

The Core Responsibilities of a Crisis Leader

Provide Clarity

In the fog of crisis, ambiguity is perilous. Leaders must distil complex situations into clear, actionable messages, even if the clarity is: "Here's what we know, here's what we don't, and here's what we're doing next."

Simplicity does not mean oversimplification. It means thoughtful communication that cuts through chaos.

Hold Emotional Space

People need their leaders to recognise the emotional reality of a crisis. This means:
- naming what's happening
- validating people's fears and experiences
- offering a sense of shared humanity.

Hiding emotions or pretending that everything is okay can harm trust. Genuine empathy fosters connection.

Make Decisive, Ethical Choices

In times of crisis, indecision breeds confusion. Leaders must be prepared to act with moral clarity and speed while remaining open to making adjustments as new information emerges.

Ethical clarity involves asking, "What is the right thing to do? What upholds dignity, fairness, and wellbeing?"

Sustain the Team

Crisis is draining. Leaders must pace their people, protect their wellbeing, and prevent burnout. This includes checking in emotionally, adjusting expectations, and celebrating small wins.

Your team's ability to function tomorrow depends on how you treat them today.

The Mindset of a Crisis Leader

Calm Is Contagious

Leaders establish the emotional tone. Panic, anxiety, or anger from the top create a ripple effect. Composure doesn't mean suppressing emotions; it means managing your state so you can be a stabilising force.

Adaptability Over Perfection

In a crisis, plans can unravel. Leaders need to be flexible, iterative, and responsive to change. The aim is not flawless execution; instead, it's about ongoing alignment with the shifting reality.

Purpose as a Compass

When uncertainty prevails, purpose serves as the anchor. Leaders who link every decision to the organisation's core mission enable people to remain focused and inspired.

Communication During Crisis

Communication is not a task in crisis; it is a lifeline. The best crisis leaders:
- communicate early and often
- are transparent about uncertainty

- avoid spin or false promises
- repeat key messages for reassurance
- allow space for questions and feedback.

Importantly, they listen as much as they speak.

Common Mistakes Leaders Make in Crisis

- ***Overconfidence:*** Pretending to have all the answers erodes credibility.
- ***Under-communicating:*** Silence breeds speculation.
- ***Overload:*** Flooding people with information creates confusion.
- ***Emotional shutdown:*** Leaders who ignore or suppress emotion become distant and ineffective.
- ***Neglecting self-care:*** Burnt-out leaders cannot lead effectively.

Being aware of these pitfalls enables leaders to navigate crises with greater intention and impact.

Crisis as a Leadership Test and Opportunity

Crisis magnifies leadership. It reveals strengths, exposes gaps, and demands growth. Yet it also creates opportunities to:

- build trust through honest communication
- model resilience and compassion
- transform systems, not just stabilise them
- strengthen the culture through shared adversity.

The leaders people remember most are those who guided them through the storm, not just those who shone in the sunshine.

Self-Leadership During Crisis

To guide others through a crisis, leaders must first guide themselves. This means:
- managing your emotional triggers
- creating space for reflection (even in chaos)
- seeking counsel, not isolation
- grounding yourself in routine, values, and relationships
- asking for help when needed.

Crisis leadership is emotionally expensive. Aim to recharge intentionally.

The Long Tail of Crisis Leadership

The formal crisis may pass, yet the emotional and organisational impact endures. Leaders must remain engaged long after the headlines fade to:
- support recovery and reflection
- evaluate what worked and what didn't
- honour those affected
- integrate lessons into future planning.

Leadership continues through and beyond crisis; closure matters.

Showing Up When It Matters Most

Leadership in a crisis isn't about being perfect. It's about being present. It's about showing up with steadiness when others feel shaken, with humility when the path is unclear, and with hope when fear takes hold.

Crisis tests your character and shapes who you become. It requires you to transition from competence to character, and from hierarchy to humanity.

So when a crisis comes, as it always does, breathe. Listen. Lead. And remember: the most enduring form of leadership is not command but care in action.

Staying Grounded Under Pressure

Pressure is a constant companion of leadership. Whether it's the weight of expectations, the urgency of a decision, or the spotlight of accountability, pressure reveals the depth and durability of a leader's inner foundation. To lead effectively under pressure is not to escape it but to stay grounded within it.

Being grounded means staying emotionally centred, mentally clear, and ethically anchored, regardless of the volatility surrounding you. It is the ability to respond rather than react, to choose values over impulses, and to lead with presence instead of panic.

Understanding Pressure

Pressure is more than just busyness or workload. It is a convergence of:

- *High stakes*: The impact of decisions affects people, performance, and outcomes.
- *Compressed time*: Urgency demands quick thinking without full context.
- *Visibility*: Leaders are watched by teams, boards, media, or the public.

- **Responsibility:** Leaders carry the burden of results and consequences.

Pressure can distort perception. It narrows focus, amplifies emotion, and triggers instinctual responses, often at the expense of strategic or ethical clarity. That's why grounding practices are vital for sustainable and effective leadership.

The Impact of Being Ungrounded

When leaders lose their grounding, the consequences ripple through the organisation.
- Emotional reactivity replaces thoughtful decision-making.
- Teams absorb the leader's stress and anxiety.
- Culture shifts toward blame, avoidance, or burnout.
- Mistakes are made, not because of poor intent, but poor presence.

An ungrounded leader may appear successful on the surface but leave behind exhaustion, confusion, and erosion of trust.

The Grounded Leader: Core Characteristics

Self-Awareness

Grounded leaders are aware of their emotional triggers, biases, and limitations. They can observe their internal state without being consumed by it.

Clarity of Values

When decisions are complex, grounded leaders turn to principles, not popularity or pressure, for guidance.

Presence

They remain emotionally and physically present, even in the face of discomfort. They don't disconnect, distract, or deflect.

Regulation

They respond with intention. They can slow down under pressure, pause before reacting, and choose their tone and timing.

Perspective

They zoom out to see the bigger picture. They separate signal from noise and urgency from importance.

Practices for Staying Grounded

Pause and Breathe

In high-pressure situations, a single mindful breath can interrupt the cycle of reactivity. It stabilises the nervous system and restores access to the prefrontal cortex, which is responsible for rational thinking.

Even a three-second pause can turn a conversation from an emotional reaction to a strategic response.

Return to Purpose

Pressure can often feel overwhelming when we lose sight of our purpose. Grounded leaders consistently reconnect with the mission, vision, or values that provide meaning to their roles.

Ask, "What matters most right now?"

Use Inner Dialogue

Grounded leaders engage in intentional self-talk.
- "You've been here before."
- "One step at a time."
- "Stay curious, not certain."

The way we speak to ourselves when under pressure shapes how we present ourselves to others.

Anchor in Routine

When external conditions are unstable, internal rituals provide stability. Grounded leaders adhere to routines for reflection, rest, movement, and connection, even in times of peak stress.

Consistency fosters calm.

Seek Perspective

In high-pressure environments, it's easy to become tunnel-visioned. Grounded leaders seek input. They ask, "What am I not seeing?" or "What would a trusted mentor say here?"

Perspective doesn't undermine authority. It enhances decision quality.

Pressure as an Opportunity for Influence

Pressure isn't just a test; it's an opportunity to lead at your best. People remember not only what leaders do in challenging moments but also how they do it. A grounded leader becomes:
- a model for emotional resilience
- a source of confidence for others
- a steadying force in chaos
- a builder of long-term trust.

Moments of pressure reveal whether a leader's presence aligns with their principles.

Avoiding the Traps of Pressure

Even experienced leaders fall into common traps under pressure:
- ***Speed over substance***: Rushing to relieve tension rather than make sound decisions.
- ***Ego over insight***: Defending pride rather than seeking truth.

- ***Control over collaboration***: Micromanaging out of fear.
- ***Avoidance over action***: Delaying or dodging hard conversations.

Being aware of these traps and having the discipline to choose differently sets grounded leaders apart from those who are reactive.

The Inner Game of Pressure

Staying grounded doesn't mean experiencing fewer emotions; it means developing greater emotional skills. Grounded leadership starts with mastering oneself and:
- recognising when pressure is building
- understanding what fear or story is being triggered
- choosing a response aligned with your best self.

Leaders who excel in the inner game remain true to their integrity, clarity, and humanity, even when the external world is in flux.

Strength Through Stillness

Staying grounded under pressure is not about being unfeeling; it's about maintaining a balanced perspective. It's about feeling fully without being ruled by those feelings. It's about knowing that intensity will rise, but so too can your capacity to meet it with grace.

Pressure is part of leadership. However, panic, reactivity, and burnout don't have to be. With discipline, reflection, and emotional intelligence, leaders can establish a strong internal foundation capable of bearing the weight of leadership.

So in moments of pressure:
- Slow down to lead forward.

- Speak with clarity and conviction.
- Return to your purpose.
- Let the calm within you become the calm around you.

Regulating Emotion in Turbulent Times

In turbulent times, leaders are not just decision-makers; they are emotional anchors. When the world outside is spinning due to crisis, change, conflict, or uncertainty, people instinctively turn to their leaders for steadiness, clarity, and reassurance. Yet leaders themselves are human, and they too experience fear, frustration, anger, and grief. The difference lies in how they respond to these emotions. At the heart of sustainable leadership in turbulence is a vital skill: emotional regulation.

Emotional regulation is not about suppressing or denying emotions; it is about managing them effectively and productively. It is the ability to recognise, manage, and direct emotional responses so they serve your values, team, and goals. It enables leaders to remain composed under stress, make informed decisions, and act as role models for resilience.

Why Emotional Regulation Matters

Leaders Set the Emotional Tone

The way a leader responds to adversity establishes the cultural standard. If they react with panic, blame, or avoidance, others are likely to mirror that response. If they remain composed, curious, and purposeful, it fosters calm and cohesion.

Unregulated Emotion Distorts Decision-Making

Strong emotions can impair judgement, leading to impulsive decisions, miscommunication, and damage to relationships. Regulated leaders can pause, assess, and respond strategically, even when the stakes are high.

Psychological Safety Depends on It

When leaders manage their emotions effectively, teams feel more secure. Emotional outbursts, passive aggression, or withdrawing from leadership responsibilities erode trust and foster anxiety.

Leadership Credibility Is Earned Through Consistency

In turbulent times, people want to know what they can expect from their leaders. Emotional regulation fosters a dependable presence that others can rely on, even in uncertain times.

Understanding Emotional Regulation

Emotional regulation involves several key processes:

- *Awareness*: Recognising your emotional state in real time
- *Labelling*: Naming the emotion accurately ("I'm anxious" vs. "I'm frustrated")
- *Pausing*: Creating space between feeling and reaction
- *Reframing*: Challenging unhelpful thoughts or assumptions
- *Redirecting*: Choosing a behaviour or response aligned with your goals.

It's a skill that can be developed through practice, rather than a personality trait that you're either born with or not.

Common Emotional Triggers for Leaders

Turbulence amplifies emotional sensitivity. Leaders frequently encounter:
- fear of failure or blame
- frustration with resistance to change
- anger at injustice or incompetence
- sadness at loss (of people, opportunity, or identity)
- anxiety about the unknown.

These are natural responses. The aim is not to avoid them but to respond with intention, rather than instinct.

Signs You're Emotionally Dysregulated

Even the strongest leaders experience moments when their emotions dominate. Warning signs include:
- reacting impulsively or aggressively
- withdrawing or shutting down emotionally
- blaming others to deflect discomfort
- avoiding necessary conversations
- feeling chronically overwhelmed or cynical.

When you notice these signs, it's time to take a break, reassess, and practice emotional regulation strategies.

Practical Tools for Regulating Emotion

The Power of the Pause

Take a moment to breathe. Even 10 to 30 seconds can interrupt an emotional surge and help the rational brain to re-engage.

Practice box breathing (inhale for 4 seconds, hold for 4 seconds, exhale for 4 seconds, hold for 4 seconds) to calm the nervous system.

Name It to Tame It

Labelling emotions helps deactivate the amygdala and reduce emotional intensity. Instead of saying, "I'm stressed," try, "I'm feeling overwhelmed because I fear losing control of the outcome."

Clarity in emotions leads to clarity in responses.

Journal or Reflect

Please take note of your feelings and the reasons behind them. This practice creates distance from the emotion, making it easier to assess objectively.

Try asking, "What's going on here?" or "What story am I telling myself?"

Shift the Narrative

Challenge distorted thoughts:
- From "I'm failing" to "This is a tough situation, and I'm doing the best I can."
- From "They're against me" to "They might be confused or afraid; what do they need?"

Reframing isn't about false positivity; it's about discovering a more accurate and helpful perspective.

Anchor in Values

When emotions surge, return to your leadership values. Ask, "How would the leader I aspire to be respond right now?"

This grounds your behaviour in character, not circumstance.

Supporting Emotional Regulation in Others

A regulated leader helps others regulate, too. In turbulent times:

- *Model calmness*: Don't fake it, but centre yourself before engaging others.
- *Create space for expression*: Encourage team members to share their concerns without fear of judgement.
- *Normalise emotion*: Remind others it's okay to feel disrupted and that emotion is not a weakness.
- *Coach through crisis*: Help people name their emotions, and to reflect and reframe when needed.

When individuals feel recognised and emotionally supported, they tend to perform better, adapt more quickly, and develop deeper trust.

Building Long-Term Emotional Resilience

Sustainable leadership requires habits that replenish your emotional capacity.

- Sleep, nutrition, and movement for physical wellbeing.
- Time in nature or solitude to reset your nervous system.
- Meaningful relationships to stay emotionally supported.
- Reflection practices (journalling, coaching, meditation) to process challenges.
- Boundaries that protect your energy from emotional overload.

Emotional regulation is easier when you're emotionally resourced.

Case Study: Emotional Regulation in Action

During the peak of the COVID-19 pandemic, many local government CEOs and frontline leaders had to make tough decisions, such as shutting down services, enforcing mandates, or delivering bad news to their communities. Those who led effectively:
- acknowledged their fear and stress
- sought support and advice, rather than isolating
- communicated transparently, even when answers were unclear
- modelled emotional steadiness while still being human
- practised daily self-regulation to avoid burnout.

Their leadership might not have been perfect, yet it was present, principled, and emotionally intelligent.

Composure Is a Leadership Superpower

In turbulent times, the leader's emotional state shapes the organisation's emotional climate. If you feel anxious, so do they. If you're calm, they draw on your steadiness. If you remain grounded, you find your footing.

Regulating emotion isn't about denying what you feel; it's about owning it, managing it, and using it for the benefit of your people and purpose. It's a muscle that grows stronger with awareness and practice.

So when the waves rise, return to your breath. Return to your values. Return to presence. You don't need to have all the answers; you need to show up with intention, courage, and clarity.

In times of turbulence, your emotional regulation is your leadership.

Having Difficult Conversations and Conflict

Leadership isn't just about setting direction, inspiring a vision, or driving outcomes; it's also about navigating tension. Conflict and tough conversations are unavoidable in any organisation where people closely collaborate. Differing perspectives, unmet expectations, emotional pressure, and competing priorities generate friction. The most effective leaders aren't those who shy away from these challenges but those who tackle them skilfully, directly, and with integrity.

Avoiding conflict often results in greater harm than the conflict itself. It allows misunderstandings to grow, resentment to accumulate, and standards to decline. Leaders need to be fluent in the language of difficult conversations. This is not a sign of harshness; it demonstrates respect, responsibility, and maturity.

Why Leaders Must Embrace Difficult Conversations

Difficult conversations are the crucible of leadership. They often involve:
- giving or receiving tough feedback
- addressing performance concerns

- resolving interpersonal tension
- communicating unwelcome decisions
- confronting breaches of values or behaviour.

Each of these moments presents a chance to strengthen culture, build trust, clarify expectations, and foster stronger relationships. However, that only occurs if they are managed with care and courage.

The Cost of Avoidance

Leaders who steer clear of conflict or challenging conversations often justify their actions as a form of kindness or diplomacy. However, the actual cost includes:

- ***Erosion of credibility***: Team members lose respect for leaders who tolerate underperformance or misalignment.
- ***Cultural drift***: Core values are compromised when violations go unaddressed.
- ***Poor morale***: High performers resent leaders who won't confront toxic behaviours or incompetence.
- ***Missed growth***: Avoiding tough feedback robs people of the chance to improve and succeed.

Avoidance isn't kindness; it's abdication. It prioritises comfort over progress.

Key Mindsets for Navigating Difficult Conversations

Curiosity Over Certainty

Engage in the conversation with the aim of understanding, rather than merely seeking to be understood. Assume there are perspectives or factors that you may not yet recognise. Curiosity can diffuse defensiveness.

Courage Over Comfort

Most tough conversations don't get easier with time. Delaying them adds to the emotional burden. Commit to engaging despite the discomfort.

Care Over Control

Approach the person with respect and a positive attitude. Aim for growth or resolution, rather than punishment or dominance.

Preparation Matters

Before initiating a difficult conversation:
- Clarify your purpose. What's the outcome you want?
- Prepare facts and examples. Be specific, not vague or accusatory.
- Reflect on your own emotions. Are you calm enough to lead constructively?
- Consider the other person's context. What might be affecting their behaviour?

A well-prepared conversation is more likely to be received with openness and clarity.

The Conversation Framework

A practical framework many leaders use is "State, Inquire, Listen, Respond".

State the issue clearly and non-defensively. Use specific observations, not generalisations.

"I've noticed that project deadlines have been consistently missed over the past three weeks."

Inquire about the other person's perspective.

"Can you help me understand what's been happening on your end?"

Listen actively and empathetically. Don't interrupt or rebut immediately.

Respond with your perspective, expectations, and next steps.

"I appreciate the challenges you're facing. At the same time, we must fulfil our commitments. Let's talk about how we can ensure that moving forward."

Handling Emotion in Conflict

Difficult conversations are inherently emotionally charged. Leaders must be prepared to manage:

- *Defensiveness*: Respond with calm curiosity.
- *Tears or anger*: Hold space; don't escalate. Offer a break if needed.
- *Projection*: Stay anchored in your values, and don't take blame-shifting personally.

Your role isn't to fix others' emotions but to create a steady space where brutal truth can be explored and respected.

Conflict as a Creative Force

Conflict is not inherently harmful. When handled well, it can:

- reveal blind spots and spark innovation
- clarify roles and expectations
- build stronger trust and respect
- align values and purpose.

Healthy teams don't eliminate conflict; they transform it into a source of growth and development.

Tips for Ongoing Conflict Management

Name issues early. The longer tension simmers, the harder it is to address constructively.

Address behaviour, not character. Focus on actions, not labels or assumptions.

Use "I" language. Own your observations and feelings.

Document agreements. Ensure clarity on what has been resolved and what is expected next.

Follow up. Accountability demonstrates that you value both the outcome and the relationship.

Cultural Considerations in Conflict

Different cultures and personalities exhibit varying conflict styles, ranging from direct to indirect. Good leaders:

- are aware of these dynamics
- tailor their approach to be both respectful and effective
- create psychologically safe environments where people feel permission to speak honestly.

Cultural awareness increases the effectiveness of difficult conversations across diverse teams.

The Leader's Role: Model and Mediator

Leaders must model constructive conflict resolution and be willing to mediate when others are unable to do so. This includes:

- creating structures for feedback and resolution
- intervening when dynamics become toxic

- coaching team members on how to navigate disagreements well.

A team's ability to thrive through challenge reflects the quality of its leadership.

The Discipline of Difficult Conversations

Difficult conversations are a leadership discipline. They require:
- emotional regulation
- clear intention
- active listening
- a bias toward resolution over avoidance.

Avoiding a conversation weakens your leadership. Engaging in one with care and courage strengthens it. Handling conflict well is not a threat to leadership; it is a testament to it.

When you speak the truth with empathy, confront issues with respect, and remain open in the face of emotion, you not only resolve problems but also foster a culture.

So steer the conversation. Embrace the discomfort. And remember: the path to stronger teams and deeper trust runs directly through the heart of honest dialogue.

Handling Confrontation, Feedback, and Emotionally Charged Moments

In leadership, not every moment is measured or methodical. Some come quickly and intensely, charged with emotion, shaped by tension, and defined by a sense of urgency. These are the crucible moments of leadership: a team member lashing out in frustration, a feedback session turning defensive, or a confrontation over values or performance. In these moments, how a leader responds speaks volumes about their emotional intelligence, values, and capacity to lead under pressure.

Dealing with confrontation, feedback, and emotionally charged moments isn't about dodging discomfort. It's about remaining composed, intentional, and human when faced with heightened emotions. This is one of the most challenging and defining aspects of leadership.

Why These Moments Matter

Leaders are not only responsible for making decisions, but they are also stewards of emotional tone. Moments of confrontation or high emotion present an opportunity to:
- deepen trust through honest engagement

- model composure and values in action
- surface and resolve underlying issues
- reinforce accountability with empathy
- turn conflict into connection.

When handled well, emotionally charged moments can become turning points in relationships, performance, and culture.

Understanding the Dynamics

Emotionally charged moments often arise when:
- expectations are misaligned
- feedback threatens identity or ego
- long-suppressed tensions erupt
- boundaries are violated
- values are in conflict.

What makes these moments difficult is not just the topic itself but also the emotions associated with it, such as fear, anger, shame, disappointment, or hurt. The leader must navigate both the issue and the emotional undercurrents it carries.

The Role of Self-Regulation

Your ability to handle the moment relies on your capability to govern yourself. Leaders must learn to:
- notice rising emotion in real time
- pause before reacting
- breathe and centre their nervous system
- stay grounded in intention, not impulse.

Your tone, body language, and emotional state can either escalate or de-escalate the moment. Manage your physiology to enhance your influence.

Dealing With Confrontation

Confrontation doesn't need to be destructive. It's a form of honesty, though it can often be clumsy or intense. Here's how to handle it appropriately.

De-escalate First, Then Engage

If someone confronts you with intensity, focus on soothing the emotional energy before discussing the facts.
- Lower your voice.
- Speak slowly.
- Validate the emotion ("I can see you're frustrated.").
- Don't match volume or aggression.

You can't reason with someone in fight-or-flight mode. Create space for emotional downshifting.

Stay Curious, Not Defensive

Even if the confrontation feels unfair, ask:
- What's behind this reaction?
- What do they need to feel heard or respected?
- What can I learn from this, even if I disagree?

Defensiveness hampers learning, while curiosity fosters connection.

Know When to Pause

If things are too hot, it's perfectly alright to say, "This is important, and I want to give it the attention it deserves. Let's take a short break and come back to this."

Time and space can help regulate emotional intensity.

Giving and Receiving Feedback Under Pressure

Feedback becomes more difficult when:
- it's unexpected

- it touches identity or self-worth
- it is delivered poorly
- the person is emotionally depleted or stressed.

To Give Feedback Well
- Be timely, specific, and grounded in observation.
- Focus on behaviour, not personality.
- Balance truth with care.
- Make it a dialogue, not a monologue.

Example:

"In yesterday's meeting, I noticed you cut off two team members. I know you're passionate, but I want us to encourage a more balanced dialogue. How do you see it?"

To Receive Feedback Well
- Breathe and listen fully before responding.
- Ask clarifying questions.
- Separate intent from impact.
- Thank the person, even if it stings.

Receiving feedback with grace under pressure is a sign of emotional maturity.

Managing Emotionally Charged Moments with Teams

These may include:
- a team member crying or becoming visibly upset
- an argument breaking out in a meeting
- someone challenging your authority or decisions in public.

In these moments:
- Acknowledge the emotion without judgement

  "I can see this has upset you. Let's take a moment."

- Offer containment without shutting down
  "Let's step aside to talk privately."
- Maintain respect for all parties involved.

Don't punish emotion. Help the team to understand it, hold it, and move forward together.

Building Skills to Handle Emotionally Difficult Interactions

Emotional Literacy: Learn to identify and articulate feelings, both your own and those of others. This helps reduce fear and defensiveness.

Boundary Setting: Assert limits when behaviour crosses boundaries, without shaming.

Empathetic Assertion: Combine empathy ("I understand you're upset") with direction ("We still need to move forward").

Practise Under Pressure: Use roleplay or coaching to prepare for high-stakes interactions.

The Value of Debriefing Difficult Moments

After a charged interaction:
- Reflect on what went well and what didn't.
- Name your own emotional experience.
- Reconnect with the other party if needed.
- Reaffirm shared goals or expectations.

Repair builds strength. Conflict doesn't ruin relationships; avoidance or mishandling does.

Great leaders do not shy away from emotional complexity; they meet it with presence, clarity, and care.

Emotional Leadership in Real Time

Emotionally charged moments are not interruptions to leadership; they are leadership. They demand:
- presence over panic
- curiosity over control
- compassion over coercion.

In these moments, you don't need to find the perfect words. You need to be grounded, open, and human.

So when the volume rises, the stakes sharpen, or the room tightens with tension, take a breath. Centre yourself. Step forward. These are the moments for which your leadership was made.

Balancing Empathy with Accountability

Empathy and accountability are often framed as opposites in leadership, one seen as soft and the other as hard. However, this presents a false dichotomy. In reality, excellent leadership requires both. Empathy without accountability leads to complacency, while accountability without empathy results in fear. Leadership that combines the two fosters cultures of trust, performance, and psychological safety.

Balancing empathy with accountability is a challenging task. It requires leaders to care deeply while also challenging directly. It involves holding people to high standards because you respect them, not in spite of it. This balance lies at the heart of emotionally intelligent leadership.

What Is Empathy?

Empathy is the ability to understand and share the feelings of others. In leadership, this manifests as:

- taking time to understand team members' perspectives
- recognising personal or emotional struggles
- adjusting communication based on individual needs

- being present in moments of difficulty or conflict.

Empathy says, "I see you. I care. I'm here."

Empathy isn't about lowering expectations; it's about honouring the humanity of those you lead.

What Is Accountability?

Accountability involves establishing clear expectations and ensuring they are fulfilled. It encompasses:
- defining roles, responsibilities, and standards
- providing honest feedback when expectations aren't met
- following through on consequences when necessary
- modelling personal responsibility and ownership.

Accountability says, "We have a job to do. Standards matter. We keep our word."

It is not punitive; it is principled. It protects culture, outcomes, and fairness.

The False Choice: Kind or Strong

Many leaders struggle to balance these forces because they believe they must choose:
- "If I hold them accountable, I'm being too harsh."
- "If I show empathy, they'll take advantage of me."

This mindset leads to one of two toxic extremes:
1. Empathy without accountability creates a permissive, vague culture where poor performance remains unchecked.
2. Accountability without empathy creates a harsh, transactional environment that undermines morale and engagement.

High-performing teams flourish in cultures where individuals feel both valued and accountable.

The Leader's Role: Compassionate Truth-Telling

The actual task of a leader is to tell the truth with compassion. This means:
- being direct without being disrespectful
- being honest without being hurtful
- addressing issues without eroding dignity.

Example:

"I understand this has been a tough quarter for you. I appreciate your effort. At the same time, we need to address the missed deadlines and discuss how we can move forward."

This approach recognises context without excusing outcomes. It combines empathy and expectation.

How to Balance Empathy and Accountability

Start With Clarity

You cannot hold someone accountable for what was never clearly defined. Empathetic leaders take the time to:
- define roles and outcomes
- explain why standards exist
- ensure understanding and buy-in.

Clarity is kindness. It helps prevent confusion and resentment in the long run.

Know the Individual

Empathy involves knowing your people.
- What motivates them?
- What challenges are they facing?
- How do they prefer to receive feedback?

Accountability is more effective when it's tailored, not one-size-fits-all.

Check Your Intent

When holding someone accountable, ask:
- Am I doing this to protect performance and culture?
- Am I showing up in a way that honours their dignity?

When showing empathy, ask:
- Am I helping this person grow?
- Am I avoiding discomfort, or acting in their best interest?

Empathy is not indulgence. Accountability is not aggression; intent matters.

Communicate Often

Don't wait for formal reviews. Offer regular, genuine feedback in real-time. Create room for both recognition and correction.

The best cultures normalise accountability and emotional expression.

What It Looks Like in Practice

Situation	Empathy-Only Approach	Accountability-Only Approach	Balanced Leadership Approach
A staff member is repeatedly late.	"They're going through a lot; I'll let it slide."	"If you're late again, you're out."	"I know mornings have been tough; let's discuss support options. However, we also need to enhance our timeliness moving forward."
A team misses a major deadline.	"They tried hard. It's okay."	"This failure is unacceptable."	"I recognise your effort and the challenges you faced. Let's review what happened and establish a plan to prevent this from happening again."
A colleague lashes out in a meeting.	"They must be stressed."	"That was completely unprofessional."	"I can see that was an emotional moment. Let's have a private chat about what happened and how we can manage these situations differently."

Empathy and Accountability in High-Stakes Moments

In times of crisis, layoffs, or significant change, leaders must increase both:
- empathy to acknowledge the human impact
- accountability is essential to progress towards stability and clarity.

The most trusted leaders during turbulent times are those who:
- speak honestly
- act consistently
- show humanity without losing resolve.

Leading With Emotional Honesty

Empathy and accountability also apply to self-leadership. This means:
- admitting your own mistakes
- being transparent about your limits
- holding yourself to the same standards you expect of others.

Emotional honesty fosters trust. It enables others to follow you, not because you're perfect but because you're genuine.

Challenges and Pitfalls

Over-Empathising
- Making excuses for poor behaviour
- Avoiding conflict to protect feelings
- Creating double standards

Over-Enforcing
- Dismissing people's struggles

- Enforcing rules without understanding context
- Believing vulnerability is weakness

Avoid the extremes. Aim for integration.

The Long-Term Impact of Balance

When leaders balance empathy with accountability, they create:

- ***Cultures of trust***: People know they'll be treated fairly and with respect.
- ***High performance***: Standards are clear, consistent, and enforced.
- ***Strong relationships***: People feel supported and challenged.
- ***Sustainable engagement***: Motivation flows from being seen, valued, and expected to rise.

People don't leave because they are held accountable. They leave when they feel disrespected, unheard, or unsupported.

Leading With Both Heart and Spine

Balancing empathy with accountability is not about compromise; it's about being whole. It's about leading with both heart and backbone.

Heart says, "I see your effort. I care about your growth."

Spine says, "We still have a job to do. I expect your best."

Together, they cultivate a leadership style that is emotionally intelligent, culturally aware, and performance-focused.

So lead with warmth and clarity. Hold space, and maintain standards. The best leaders don't choose between empathy and accountability; they embody both.

The Emotional Culture of a Team

Every team has a culture. Most leaders view it in terms of values, rules, or behaviours, but beneath that lies something equally significant and often overlooked: emotional culture. This concept pertains to the shared emotional life of a team, encompassing how individuals feel, express, and respond to emotions in the workplace. It includes which emotions are encouraged and which are suppressed, as well as how emotional energy flows within the group.

Emotional culture shapes motivation, resilience, communication, and trust. It influences whether people feel safe to speak up, whether they bring their whole selves to work, and whether they recover quickly from setbacks or retreat into silence. In high-performing teams, emotional culture is not a matter of chance; it's intentionally nurtured.

What Is Emotional Culture?

Unlike cognitive culture values, norms, and beliefs, emotional culture pertains to the feelings regarded as acceptable, appropriate, or unwelcome within a group.

It addresses questions such as:
- Is it okay to show vulnerability?
- Do people feel safe admitting mistakes?
- Are enthusiasm, joy, or humour welcome?
- How is anger or disappointment handled?
- Is conflict engaged with or avoided?

Emotional culture is rarely written down, but it's deeply felt. It is communicated through tone of voice, facial expressions, body language, and reactions to emotion. It lives in the day-to-day emotional climate of the team.

Why Emotional Culture Matters

It Affects Performance

A positive emotional culture, characterised by warmth, safety, and optimism, enhances engagement, creativity, and collaboration. In contrast, a negative culture, marked by fear, blame, or indifference, suppresses initiative and performance.

It Drives Retention and Wellbeing

People don't just leave toxic bosses; they depart from emotionally toxic environments. Emotional culture affects whether individuals feel seen, valued, and supported.

It Shapes Team Resilience

Teams with strong emotional cultures tend to bounce back more quickly. They support one another, recover from conflicts, and sustain their energy during challenging times.

Types of Emotional Cultures

Research identifies a range of emotional cultures, but some common types include:

- *Caring Culture*: Empathy, kindness, and support are prioritised. Strong relational bonds and high psychological safety.
- *Joyful Culture*: Laughter, celebration, and enthusiasm are common. Boosts morale and energy.
- *Fearful Culture*: Mistakes are punished, and people feel anxious. Leads to defensiveness and silence.
- *Aggressive Culture*: Competition and dominance are valued. Can drive results but damage trust.
- *Apathetic Culture*: Emotion is suppressed. People are disengaged or checked out.

Teams often consist of a mix of these but typically one type prevails.

How Emotional Culture Develops

Policies do not set emotional culture; it is shaped by:
- leaders' emotional expression and behaviour
- peer modelling and reinforcement
- reactions to emotional events (e.g. mistakes, conflict, success)
- team rituals, language, and norms.

For instance, when a team shares laughter and celebrates success together, joy becomes an integral part of the culture. Conversely, if individuals are ridiculed for expressing doubt or sadness, vulnerability is suppressed.

The Hidden Messages of Culture

Every team sends emotional signals, often unintentionally. Consider:
- Are people celebrated for their hustle but criticised for seeking help?

- Is disagreement encouraged or shunned?
- Do leaders express their emotions or solely exhibit authority?

These micro-messages accumulate to create a clear emotional picture, which shapes how people behave, voice their opinions, and support one another.

Signs of a Healthy Emotional Culture

- People feel comfortable sharing challenges or mistakes.
- There's space for humour and joy alongside hard work.
- Feedback is given and received constructively.
- Emotional check-ins or acknowledgments are normalised.
- Emotions are neither exaggerated nor suppressed; they're respected.

In these environments, people don't leave parts of themselves at the door. They bring their complete emotional intelligence to the task.

Signs of a Toxic or Weak Emotional Culture

- Team members avoid hard conversations.
- Discomfort or dissent is met with withdrawal or punishment.
- People feel like they must wear a mask at work.
- There's high turnover or silent disengagement.
- Emotions are either constantly explosive or completely absent.

These cultures may survive, but they seldom thrive. They depend on fear, compliance, or routine rather than connection, resilience, or energy.

The Leader's Role in Emotional Culture

Leaders shape emotional culture through:
- *Their emotional habits*: What do they express? What do they suppress?
- *Their reactions to others' emotions*: Are they validating or dismissive?
- *The norms they reinforce*: Do they reward honesty and vulnerability? Do they shut down emotional expression?

The leader's emotional presence acts as a cultural thermostat. If they allow space for emotion, others will too. If they suppress it, it establishes a tone of emotional risk.

Building a Strong Emotional Culture

Name It

Talk about emotions openly. Ask your team:
- How do we want to feel at work?
- What emotions help us do our best work?
- What's getting in the way?

Establishing a common language about emotions enhances awareness and intention.

Model It

Be the emotional culture you want to see. If you wish to be open, show vulnerability. If you want to be optimistic, express hope. If you want accountability, own your mistakes.

Reinforce It

Call out moments that reflect the emotional culture you're building.

"Thanks for raising that concern; honesty strengthens our team."

Also, address moments that contradict it.

Create Rituals

Small practices build emotional culture.
- Begin meetings with check-ins.
- Celebrate small wins.
- Use humour to release tension.
- Hold space after hard conversations or decisions.

Rituals make emotion part of the rhythm of team life.

The Payoff: Performance With Humanity

A strong emotional culture doesn't entail avoiding difficult conversations or tough decisions. Instead, it involves approaching them with care, transparency, and emotional intelligence. It fosters:
- trust
- motivation
- adaptability
- retention
- collective wellbeing.

In today's workplace, where uncertainty, change, and pressure are the norm, an emotional culture is not a luxury; it is a leadership imperative.

Culture You Can Feel

Emotional culture is not something you can measure on a dashboard, but you can feel it the moment you walk into a room. It's the difference between a team that operates with fear and fatigue versus one that moves with purpose, compassion, and resilience.

As a leader, your most powerful tool in shaping emotional culture is your behaviour. Be conscious of what you're creating, what you're permitting, and what you're modelling. Ultimately, emotional culture isn't just about how people feel at work; it's also about how they remember you.

How a Leader's Emotions Set the Tone

Leadership is not just about strategy, decision-making, or vision; it is also profoundly emotional. The emotional state of a leader ripples through an organisation in both visible and invisible ways. From tone of voice in meetings to facial expressions in times of crisis, leaders constantly transmit emotion. Whether they mean to or not, their mood becomes contagious. Their calm reassures. Their anxiety spreads. Their optimism inspires. Their cynicism corrodes.

This is the emotional contagion of leadership: the science-backed phenomenon that those around them absorb a leader's emotions. A leader sets the tone not only with their words and actions but also through their emotional presence.

Why Emotional Tone Matters

People Look to the Leader First

In moments of uncertainty, people look to the leader for cues. A calm leader signals, "We've got this." A tense or distant leader signals, "Something's wrong."

Emotion Impacts Performance

Emotional tone affects cognitive function. Positive emotional climates promote higher creativity, better problem-solving, and enhanced collaboration. Negative tones, particularly when sustained, reduce risk tolerance, undermine trust, and diminish performance.

Emotion Builds or Breaks Culture

Culture is shaped by what is repeated. If a leader consistently demonstrates empathy, resilience, and authenticity, these qualities become cultural norms within their organisation. If they model reactivity, fear, or detachment, the same applies.

The Leader as an Emotional Barometer

Leaders are constantly being watched, even when they don't realise it. People notice:

- the leader's mood when they walk into the room
- how they respond to bad news
- how they talk about the future
- whether they seem open or closed off.

These micro-signals act as team barometers. They subtly convey what is safe, what is valued, and what is expected.

Unconscious Emotional Transmission

Many leaders underestimate how their emotional transparency is conveyed through tension in the jaw, clipped responses, and an unfocused stare, which signal far more than they intend. A leader might say, "I'm fine," but their body language says otherwise. Teams often sense the emotional truth before the verbal explanation.

This can be especially damaging when there's a mismatch between words and emotion. Leaders who preach transparency but project guardedness create confusion. Leaders who say, "We're doing great" while radiating tension invite distrust.

The Shadow Side of Emotional Tone

When a leader is unaware or unregulated in their emotions, they create unintended consequences.

- Anxious leaders create anxious teams, even when work is going well.
- Angry leaders cause people to walk on eggshells, stifling honest conversation.
- Avoidant leaders foster cultures of silence or passive conflict.
- Overly optimistic leaders can suppress necessary criticism or make others feel dismissed.

What a leader doesn't manage emotionally, others absorb.

Intentional Emotional Leadership

Great leaders recognise that their emotional tone is a tool, and they learn to use it consciously.

Self-Awareness

Ask yourself regularly:
- How am I feeling right now?
- What emotional tone am I giving off?
- Is it helping or hindering the team?

Leaders who cannot name their emotions risk being ruled by them.

Emotional Transparency

This doesn't mean emotional oversharing. It means being honest about your internal state when appropriate.

> "This is a tough moment, and I'm feeling the weight of it. But I'm committed to leading us through it."

Vulnerability, when coupled with clarity, builds trust.

Emotional Regulation

Before walking into a room, ask:
- What emotional energy do I want to bring?
- What does the team need from me right now?

Take a moment to breathe, ground yourself, and choose your emotional posture.

Leading Through Emotionally Charged Moments

When stress is high during crises, restructuring, failure, or conflict, the leader's emotional tone matters more than ever.

In these moments:
- stay calm, even if uncertain
- be honest, but not catastrophic
- acknowledge emotion without losing direction.

Say: "This is hard, and it's okay to feel that. We will get through it together."

Emotional leadership doesn't mean eliminating emotions; it means creating space for them without being overwhelmed by them.

Tone Setting in Day-to-Day Leadership

Emotional tone isn't just for high-stakes moments. It's shaped in daily habits such as:

- starting meetings with warmth and clarity
- giving feedback with empathy
- listening with presence
- responding to mistakes with curiosity, not blame.

The cumulative effect of these moments determines whether individuals feel safe, energised, and committed or guarded, indifferent, and fatigued.

What to Watch For in Yourself

Leaders should pay attention to:

- ***Default emotional states***: Do you arrive feeling anxious, impatient, or flat?
- ***Common triggers***: What types of situations make you tighten, withdraw, or become reactive?
- ***Recovery rituals***: How do you reset after emotional strain? Do you debrief, rest, reflect, or distract yourself?

Emotional self-care isn't selfish; it's essential preparation for leading others with integrity.

Emotions as Strategic Tools

Emotionally intelligent leaders know how to use emotion to influence culture and behaviour.

- Excitement can energise teams before a big launch.
- Calmness can slow panic during uncertainty.
- Compassion can restore trust after a mistake.
- Resolve can inspire commitment during a hard change.

The goal isn't to manipulate, but to lead intentionally.

Case Example: The Power of a Leader's Tone

Imagine two team leaders responding to a failed project.

Leader A walks in, flustered and irritable:
> "I don't know how this happened. I'm extremely disappointed."

Leader B enters, grounded and reflective:
> "We didn't hit the mark, and that's frustrating. However, this presents an opportunity to learn and improve our operational practices."

Same event. Different tone. Significantly different effect on morale, engagement, and next steps.

Leadership Is Emotional

At its core, leadership is about relationships, and relationships are emotional. The leader's ability to manage their emotional tone shapes everything.

- How safe people feel.
- How honest people are.
- How resilient a team becomes.
- How closely values align with culture.

You don't have to be perfectly positive all the time. But you do need to be emotionally aware, intentional, and grounded. Your presence is your power. Your tone is your signal. Your well-managed emotions are one of the most essential leadership tools you possess.

Creating a Resilient, Open, and Safe Team Environment

In today's complex, fast-paced, and often unpredictable workplaces, one of the most important things a leader can create is a resilient, open, and psychologically safe team environment. This is not just a "nice-to-have"; it's a strategic necessity. Teams that are emotionally resilient, honest in communication, and psychologically safe are more innovative, adaptive, and loyal. They learn from failure, navigate change more effectively, and perform at higher levels over time.

Resilience, openness, and safety don't emerge by chance. They must be cultivated intentionally by leaders who understand that the emotional culture of a team, how people feel, how they connect, and how they recover, matters as much as strategy or skill.

What Is a Psychologically Safe Team Environment?

Psychological safety means that people feel:
- comfortable being themselves at work
- safe to speak up with ideas, questions, or concerns
- free from fear of embarrassment, punishment, or retribution.

It's not about the absence of conflict or accountability. Instead, it's about creating a climate in which people feel they can engage honestly and constructively, even when the stakes are high.

Dr. Amy Edmondson, who popularised the concept, defines psychological safety as "a belief that one will not be punished or humiliated for speaking up with ideas, questions, concerns, or mistakes."[6]

What Is Team Resilience?

Team resilience is the collective ability of a group to recover from setbacks, adapt to change, and keep moving forward in the face of challenges. It depends not just on individual grit but on team dynamics, including:
- shared optimism and purpose
- strong relational support
- clear communication in stress
- constructive responses to failure.

Resilient teams don't avoid difficulty; they grow through it.

Why Leaders Must Build This Environment

A team may be technically skilled, well-resourced, and highly driven, but if the emotional climate is fragile, closed, or unsafe, their performance will suffer.

Without safety:
- people hide mistakes
- innovation is stifled

---

6. chrome-extension://efaidnbmnnnibpcajpcglclefindmkaj/https://www.apsc.gov.au/sites/default/files/2023-08/SES%20performance%20leadership%20framework%20-%20Integrity%20and%20psychological%20safety%20for%20leaders.pdf

- feedback loops break down
- trust fractures under pressure.

Without openness:
- candour is replaced by politeness or silence
- conflict is buried rather than resolved
- teams underperform and under-communicate.

Without resilience:
- small disruptions cause major derailments
- energy drains quickly
- burnout spreads.

A leader's ability to build the proper environment is foundational to long-term success.

Key Elements of a Safe, Open, and Resilient Team Environment

Trust as the Foundation

Trust is the glue that holds teams together. It is built through:
- reliability (doing what you say you'll do)
- integrity (acting with honesty and fairness)
- vulnerability (being open about mistakes or uncertainty).

Trust grows in consistency. It breaks in contradiction.

Clarity of Purpose and Expectations

Teams feel safer and more resilient when:
- they understand the "why" behind decisions
- expectations are transparent and fair
- roles and responsibilities are well defined.

Ambiguity erodes confidence. Clarity empowers.

Open, Two-Way Communication

Create space for honest dialogue.
- Invite feedback regularly.
- Respond without defensiveness.
- Model active listening.
- Make it safe to challenge ideas respectfully.

Communication should be an open loop, not a top-down monologue.

Emotional Honesty and Empathy

People should feel they can bring their whole selves to work, not just a curated, emotionless version of themselves. Leaders create teams that are more emotionally attuned, present, and committed when they:
- acknowledge emotion
- validate concerns
- show empathy without fixing everything.

Normalising Mistakes and Learning

Resilient teams don't punish failure; they learn from it. Leaders can:
- conduct blameless post-mortems
- acknowledge and share their missteps
- reinforce learning as a path to growth.

When failure becomes part of the learning process, rather than a source of shame, risk-taking and creativity increase.

Practices That Foster Safety, Openness, and Resilience

Psychological Safety Check-ins

Start meetings with a simple question such as:

- Is there anything we need to talk about before we get into the agenda?
- What's one word to describe how you're feeling today?

Small moments of honesty build connection and trust.

Leader Vulnerability

Model what openness looks like:

> "I feel uncertain about how this change will unfold, but I believe in our team's ability to handle it."

This demonstrates strength through honesty, not despite it.

Encourage Constructive Dissent

Say explicitly:

- I want to hear what might not be working.
- Who sees this differently?

Inviting dissent reduces groupthink and deepens dialogue.

Debrief Challenges Openly

After challenging projects or crises, reflect together:

- What went well?
- What didn't?
- What will we do differently next time?

This creates shared meaning and emotional closure.

What Undermines Safety and Resilience

- Blame culture
- Leader inconsistency or emotional volatility
- Ignoring conflict
- Micro-management or control
- Lack of follow-through on feedback
- Unspoken rules against expressing disagreement

These dynamics train people to stay silent, play small, or withdraw emotionally.

The Role of Boundaries and Accountability

A common misconception is that psychological safety means avoiding difficult conversations. Actually, it encourages them.

High safety + low accountability = comfort culture
Low safety + high accountability = fear culture
High safety + high accountability = growth culture

The leader's role is to maintain this balance.
"We care about you. And we hold you to a high standard."
That's what drives growth and wellbeing.

Building Team Rituals and Norms

Resilient, safe cultures are reinforced by:
- *Rituals*: Celebrate weekly achievements, moments of gratitude, and pulse surveys.
- *Norms*: Avoid interrupting, assume positive intent, and give permission to challenge.
- *Language*: "It's okay not to be okay; let's learn from this."

Culture develops through repetition.

A Real-World Example

Consider a team overseeing a significant organisational change. The leader:
- holds weekly check-ins for emotional temperature
- names the emotional reality: "This is stressful, and some grief is normal"

- celebrates micro-wins along the way
- opens the floor for concerns and dissent
- offers coaching and peer support options.

The result: instead of descending into chaos or burnout, the team adapts, stays connected, and moves forward with purpose. That's emotional leadership in action.

The Leader as Emotional Architect

You don't need to address every emotional problem. You don't have to protect your team from every stressor. However, it's essential to create an environment where people can confront those challenges together, with honesty, strength, and a sense of connection.

Creating a resilient, open, and psychologically safe team environment isn't just a tick-box exercise; it's a commitment. It's a daily act of leadership, where emotional culture, clear values, and intentional behaviour converge to create something more substantial than any individual: a team that thrives through challenges, not despite them.

Personal Reflection: The Real Work of Emotional Leadership

Some of the most defining moments in my leadership journey didn't happen in boardrooms or strategy sessions. They took place in quiet, emotionally charged moments that required more than just decisions; they demanded my presence.

I've led through crises when the pressure was relentless and the stakes were high. In those moments, what mattered most wasn't having all the answers; it was how I appeared. I learned that emotional steadiness is contagious. If I could stay calm, others could find their footing. That meant managing my fear, frustration, and fatigue, not by suppressing them but by recognising them privately and choosing a composed, grounded response publicly. Leadership under pressure is less about power and more about poise.

I've also found that conflict tests emotional maturity. There were chats I dreaded, ones where I feared I'd be misunderstood or that talking about behaviour would harm relationships. But avoiding those chats always costs more in the long run. When I finally leaned in with empathy, clarity, and respect, I saw that most people respond well to truth when it's delivered without ego. And often, those tough chats became turning points, building more trust, not less.

But the most humbling lesson has been about emotional culture. You can't delegate culture. You model it. I've seen firsthand how my tone, energy, and emotional habits ripple through a team. When I rushed, they became anxious. When I listened, they opened up. When I admitted mistakes, they felt safe to do the same. Emotional mastery isn't about perfection; it's about intentionality.

This part of the leadership journey, working with emotions in real time, in genuine relationships, is where the actual work resides. It's not always obvious. It doesn't attract applause. But it's what shapes teams that perform under pressure, relationships built on trust, and leaders who leave a legacy well beyond outcomes.

Because leadership, at its core, is emotional labour. And it's worth every bit of effort.

PART FOUR

Sustaining the Emotional Journey

Self-Compassion and Recovery

Leadership is demanding. It requires decision-making under pressure, emotional labour, responsibility for others' well-being, and constant adaptation to change. Yet in the face of all this, many leaders show compassion to everyone except themselves. They push through fatigue, ignore their own needs, and hold themselves to unforgiving standards, all in the name of strength, commitment, or service.

But this self-neglect comes at a cost: physical health suffers, emotional resilience erodes, and judgement becomes clouded. To lead effectively over the long term, leaders must learn to practise self-compassion and intentional recovery. These are not signs of weakness; they are disciplines of sustainable leadership.

What Is Self-Compassion?

Self-compassion, as defined by Dr. Kristin Neff[7,8], involves three key elements:

---

7. https://self-compassion.org/what-is-self-compassion/
8. https://selfcompassion.web.unc.edu/what-is-self-compassion/the-three-components-of-self-compassion/

1. ***Self-kindness***: Treating yourself with care and understanding, rather than harsh self-judgement.
2. ***Common humanity***: Recognising that imperfection and struggle are part of the shared human experience.
3. ***Mindfulness***: Observing your thoughts and feelings without suppressing or exaggerating them.

In leadership, self-compassion means:
- allowing yourself to be human
- responding to failure with learning, not self-criticism
- taking emotional rest seriously
- accepting that you can't, and don't have to, get everything right.

The Inner Critic vs. the Compassionate Coach

Most leaders possess an inner voice that critiques every decision and every misstep.
- "You should have seen this coming."
- "You're letting everyone down."
- "Why can't you handle more?"

This voice may seem to enhance performance, but over time, it fosters shame, rigidity, and burnout. Self-compassion replaces the inner critic with an inner coach:
- "That was a hard call. You did your best with what you knew."
- "It's okay to feel disappointed; let's reflect and grow."
- "You're not alone in this."

Leaders who show the same grace to themselves that they extend to others are more balanced, grounded, and emotionally available.

Recovery: The Often-Neglected Leadership Discipline

In physical training, recovery is crucial for growth. Muscles require time to repair, replenish, and adapt. Leadership is no different. The mental and emotional demands of leading necessitate intentional recovery for restoration of:
- focus and clarity
- emotional regulation
- energy and motivation
- creativity and decision-making.

Yet many leaders skip recovery entirely. They move from one crisis or task to the next, treating rest as a reward instead of a requirement. This short-term heroism leads to long-term depletion.

Types of Recovery for Leaders

Physical Recovery:
- Sleep, hydration, nutrition, exercise
- Taking breaks from screens and constant stimulation

Emotional Recovery:
- Processing difficult conversations or decisions
- Talking with a coach, mentor, or therapist
- Allowing space to feel and not just perform

Mental Recovery:
- Time away from problem-solving
- Activities that absorb attention in a non-productive way (reading, hobbies, nature)

Spiritual Recovery:
- Reconnecting with purpose
- Time for reflection, solitude, or connection to something greater than yourself

Each type of recovery strengthens the others. Together, they foster emotional renewal and cultivate a sustainable presence.

Why Leaders Resist Self-Compassion and Recovery

Fear of Appearing Weak

Many leaders equate self-care with softness. They worry that taking a break or admitting a struggle signals a lack of resilience.

Reality: Leaders who model healthy self-compassion set the tone for the team to do the same. Vulnerability earns trust, not contempt.

Overidentification with Role

Some leaders identify themselves entirely with their role. If they're not performing, they feel worthless.

Reality: You are not your title. You are a human being first, and humans need care.

High Achievement Conditioning

Driven leaders frequently emerge from environments that value perfectionism, excessive work, or the suppression of emotions.

Reality: Long-term performance requires rhythms, not merely grinding. Recovery enhances achievement.

The Cost of Neglecting Self-Compassion

When leaders ignore their own emotional needs, the results include:
- burnout
- decision fatigue
- emotional reactivity

- decreased creativity
- isolation
- loss of meaning or joy in the work.

Eventually, the very traits that made them effective, clarity, courage, and connection, become compromised.

Practising Self-Compassion in Daily Leadership

Here's how leaders can build this habit.

Create Micro-Moments of Self-Kindness

- *Before a meeting*: "What do I need right now to show up well?"
- *After a setback*: "What would I say to a colleague in this situation?"
- *In reflection*: "What am I learning from this?"

Build Recovery into Your Routine

- Allocate time for breaks in your calendar.
- Schedule time after emotionally taxing events.
- Value sleep and downtime as you would critical meetings.

Use Self-Compassion Language

Shift from:

- "I should be doing more" to "I'm doing what I can with what I have"
- "I messed that up" to "That didn't go as planned, but it's an opportunity to grow"

The Link Between Self-Compassion and Leadership Effectiveness

Studies show that self-compassionate leaders are:

- less reactive under stress
- more adaptable to change
- better able to learn from feedback
- more emotionally available to others.

It's not indulgent; it's strategic. It safeguards the leader, enabling them to defend the mission.

What Teams Learn from Leaders Who Practise Self-Compassion

When leaders are open about their need for rest, reflection, and recovery, it teaches the team that:
- wellbeing is valued
- mistakes are part of growth
- resilience includes rest, not just effort.

It invites a culture of balance and emotional maturity, one where people can be human without penalty.

Leading With Grace and Endurance

Leadership is a long game. The weight of responsibility, the pressure of visibility, and the emotional labour of serving others cannot be borne forever without a break. Self-compassion is about remaining intact, not just as a leader, but as a human being.

So allow yourself to pause. Show yourself the same kindness you extend to your team. Make recovery a part of your rhythm. Sustainable leadership doesn't stem from perfection; it arises from presence, self-respect, and a sense of grace.

Avoiding Burnout

Leadership often carries an invisible weight: the weight of expectations, the weight of decisions, and the weight of responsibility for people, performance, and culture. Over time, this weight can accumulate into something perilous: burnout.

Burnout isn't merely feeling tired after a long week. It involves emotional exhaustion, chronic detachment, and a diminished sense of impact that gradually erodes your effectiveness, health, and joy in leadership. It occurs when effort consistently outstrips recovery, and it's becoming increasingly common among leaders who view their role as a calling, not just a job.

Avoiding burnout isn't about doing less; it's about doing more effectively. It's about doing things differently. It's about establishing rhythms, boundaries, and support systems that ensure your leadership is sustainable, not sacrificial.

What Is Burnout?

The World Health Organisation defines burnout as a syndrome resulting from chronic workplace stress that has not been managed successfully. It comprises three key dimensions:

1. ***Exhaustion***: feeling depleted, drained, or unable to recover
2. ***Cynicism/detachment***: withdrawing mentally or emotionally from your role
3. ***Reduced efficacy***: doubting your ability to make a difference or perform well.

In leadership, burnout often presents subtly at first as:
- loss of joy or excitement about the work
- emotional numbness or irritability
- trouble concentrating or making decisions
- resentment of people or demands you used to enjoy.

If left unchecked, it can lead to disengagement and health problems, and can ultimately result in withdrawal from leadership altogether.

Why Leaders Are Especially Prone to Burnout

Leaders face a unique combination of stressors such as:
- constant decision-making under pressure
- holding emotional space for others while suppressing their own
- high visibility and little room to fail publicly
- long hours, blurred boundaries, and reactive schedules
- the "always on" expectation, even outside of work hours.

They are also less likely to admit to struggling or seeking help due to perceived expectations of strength, composure, and certainty.

The Early Warning Signs

Catching burnout early is crucial. Warning signs include:

- chronic fatigue despite rest
- withdrawing from relationships (at work or home)
- loss of motivation or inspiration
- increasing reliance on caffeine, alcohol, or stimulants
- avoiding difficult conversations or decisions
- feeling trapped, hopeless, or apathetic.

These are not moral failures; they are emotional red flags. They signal a need for adjustment, not more effort.

Leadership Myths That Fuel Burnout

Myth 1: "I have to be available all the time."

Truth: Constant accessibility erodes your focus, energy, and presence. You're more valuable when you're rested and present than when you're spread thin.

Myth 2: "My team needs me to be strong, always."

Truth: Authentic leadership includes vulnerability. Admitting your humanity permits others to care for theirs.

Myth 3: "Once we get through this period, it'll ease up."

Truth: If stress is structural, the "crunch" never ends. You must design systems and habits that make the pace sustainable now.

Proactive Strategies to Prevent Burnout

Avoiding burnout requires intention. It's not just about reducing workload; it's about rethinking how you lead, rest, and relate to your role.

Redesign Your Schedule for Recovery

- Block out non-negotiable recovery time (daily, weekly, monthly).

- Avoid stacking emotionally intense meetings back-to-back.
- Protect time for deep work, not just responsive work.

Your calendar reflects your values. Treat recovery as essential, not extra.

Clarify Your Boundaries

- Decide when and how you're accessible outside of work hours.
- Turn off notifications during rest periods.
- Communicate your boundaries clearly to your team.

Boundaries aren't barriers; they're conditions for sustainable contribution.

Delegate With Trust

Burnout often stems from over-responsibility. Ask:

- What am I doing that someone else is capable of?
- What am I afraid to let go of and why?

Empowering others is not abandonment. It's leadership development.

Reconnect With Purpose

Burnout can blur your sense of why. Regularly reconnect with:

- the people your leadership impacts
- the mission or outcomes you care about
- your values and legacy.

Meaning fuels resilience.

Building a Personal Burnout Buffer

Develop a personal system that includes:

- physical self-care (movement, nutrition, sleep)

- mental recovery (hobbies, silence, nature)
- emotional outlets (journalling, coaching, therapy)
- Relational support (trusted peers, mentors, family)

Leadership should not be a solo endurance event. Make connection part of your rhythm.

Crisis Mode vs. Chronic Overdrive

High-stress periods can be occasional, but what truly burns leaders out is when every day feels like a fire to put out. Ask yourself:
- Am I leading in crisis mode by default?
- When was the last time I felt restored?
- Am I reacting to pressure or shaping my own pace?

You can't lead from a place of clarity if you're constantly surviving.

Cultural Shifts to Prevent Burnout

If you're in a position of influence, model a culture that resists burnout.
- Normalise recovery, breaks, and boundaries.
- Reward output and creativity, not just busyness.
- Make emotional wellbeing part of performance conversations.

Culture is not what you say; it's what you reward and repeat.

What to Do If You're Already Burned Out

If burnout has taken hold:
- Speak to someone, a coach, mentor, GP, or mental health professional.

- Take a step back if needed (mental health leave is legitimate).
- Rebuild slowly, with minor changes before major ones.
- Let go of guilt; rest is not quitting—it's resetting.

Recovering from burnout requires time and attention, but it is certainly achievable. Leadership after experiencing burnout tends to be more insightful, modest, and grounded.

Burnout Is a Leadership Risk, Not a Badge of Honour

Burnout is not a sign that you care too much; it's a sign that you've borne too much for too long without the support structures, recovery, and self-kindness that leadership demands. It is not a measure of strength to push yourself past the point of health. True strength lies in creating a rhythm that allows you to consistently show up for your team, your mission, and yourself.

Sustainable leadership isn't about doing more; it's about doing well for long enough to matter. And that starts with protecting your most valuable leadership asset: you.

Emotional Self-Care for Sustained Leadership

Leadership is emotionally demanding. It involves managing not only your own emotions but also those of others. It requires staying calm under pressure, being present for those in distress, maintaining optimism in uncertain times, and absorbing the emotional energy of your team. Over time, this emotional output, if not balanced by intentional input, leads to depletion.

This is why emotional self-care is essential for sustained leadership. It's not a luxury or a sign of indulgence. It's the deliberate practice of attending to your inner world so you can continue to lead with clarity, compassion, and integrity. Without it, leaders risk emotional fatigue, breakdowns in decision-making, and the erosion of empathy, which undermines team trust and cohesion.

What Is Emotional Self-Care?

Emotional self-care refers to practices that help leaders:
- acknowledge and process their emotions
- regulate their responses under stress

- maintain emotional availability and presence
- rebuild emotional capacity after difficult events.

It extends beyond basic rest or relaxation. Emotional self-care is both restorative and reflective. It assists leaders in understanding their feelings, recognising why it matters, and maintaining emotional balance to serve others better.

Why Emotional Self-Care Is Often Neglected

Leaders often neglect their emotional needs for several reasons:
- They prioritise the needs of others first, always.
- They fear appearing weak or uncomposed.
- They've been conditioned to push through discomfort.
- They mistake emotional detachment for resilience.

The result is a subtle and steady loss of self-awareness. Leaders start to function on emotional autopilot, reacting rather than responding, enduring instead of leading, and suppressing instead of engaging.

The Cost of Ignoring Emotional Needs

Without emotional self-care, leaders risk:
- ***Emotional exhaustion:*** A sense of inner emptiness and overwhelm
- ***Compassion fatigue:*** Diminished capacity to care, connect, or empathise
- ***Emotional reactivity:*** Escalating conflict, defensiveness, or withdrawal
- ***Poor judgement:*** Impaired decision-making and relational missteps
- ***Disconnection:*** A growing gap between how a leader feels and how they show up

Ultimately, leaders who overlook their emotional wellbeing forfeit the very qualities that render them effective: empathy, presence, and perspective.

Core Practices of Emotional Self-Care

Emotional Check-Ins

Ask yourself regularly:
- What am I feeling right now?
- What's beneath that emotion?
- What do I need that I'm not giving myself?

These questions help you process emotions before they accumulate or explode.

Reflection and Emotional Journalling

Make space to write about:
- emotional highs and lows from the week
- patterns you're noticing in your reactions
- the emotional weight of recent decisions or conflicts.

Expressing emotions in language gives them form, allowing for insight and release.

Name and Normalise Difficult Emotions

Instead of pushing away discomfort:
- *Acknowledge it*: "I'm feeling disappointed and a bit ashamed."
- *Normalise it*: "This is a human response to a hard situation."
- *Move through it*: "What do I need to process and move forward?"

Leaders who label emotions tend to manage them more effectively.

Regular Emotional Debriefs

After challenging meetings or events:
- Pause to decompress before rushing to the next task.
- Talk it through with a trusted advisor or peer.
- Ask, "What did I carry from that conversation that I need to let go of?"

This helps stop emotional residue from building up.

Build Emotional Recovery into Your Calendar

Just like physical fatigue, emotional strain needs recovery:
- Block white space after intense meetings.
- Schedule walking meetings, nature breaks, or quiet time.
- Make space for joy and connection, not just output and productivity.

Leadership is maintained by a restorative rhythm, rather than by constant urgency.

Building Emotional Boundaries

Healthy leaders have clear emotional boundaries. They:
- recognise what is theirs to hold, and what belongs to others
- don't internalise everyone's distress
- say no to emotional labour that drains their reserves unnecessarily.

Emotional boundaries safeguard empathy. They allow leaders to empathise deeply without becoming overwhelmed by the pain or conflict of others.

Cultivating Emotional Allies

You don't have to do emotional self-care alone. Leaders benefit from:
- mentors who provide perspective and wisdom
- peer leaders who understand the unique emotional load
- coaches or therapists who offer space to explore deeper emotions.

These relationships create mirrors: spaces where leaders can be seen, heard, and emotionally supported.

Signs of Healthy Emotional Self-Care

When leaders practise emotional self-care consistently, it shows up in their leadership.
- They remain calm during conflict.
- They model healthy emotional expression.
- They bounce back quickly from stress or setbacks.
- They inspire trust through authenticity.
- They connect with their team with empathy, not obligation.

This creates emotional safety and cohesion across the team.

Organisational Impact of Leader Emotional Health

Leaders who manage their emotions also influence:
- ***Team wellbeing:*** Emotionally grounded leaders create emotionally grounded teams.
- ***Retention:*** People stay where they feel seen, understood, and supported.
- ***Culture:*** The way a leader handles emotion becomes a blueprint for others.

Emotional self-care is not only a personal practice; it's a cultural signal.

Balancing Toughness with Tenderness

Outstanding leadership blends tough-mindedness and warm-heartedness. Emotional self-care allows both.
- It preserves emotional stamina for hard conversations.
- It keeps compassion alive through fatigue.
- It helps leaders stay steady without becoming detached.

This balance earns trust, fosters safety, and makes courage sustainable.

Ritualising Emotional Self-Care

Make emotional self-care part of your leadership rhythm, not just a crisis response.
- Start or end your day with 10 minutes of reflection.
- Choose a weekly ritual for emotional reset (walk, journal, mentor call).
- Create a monthly check-in with a trusted peer or coach.

Over time, these rituals shape resilience and maturity.

Lead With Fullness, Not Emptiness

Leadership that endures is leadership that's emotionally nourished. Your team requires your insight and decisiveness, but they also need your humanity. And you require your care.

Emotional self-care involves consistently engaging, rather than merely going through the motions. It's how you remain grounded amidst turmoil, connected in times of conflict, and compassionate in the long run.

So check in with yourself. Honour what you feel. Create space to rest, release, and recover because the emotional sustainability of your leadership starts with how you lead yourself.

Growth and Reflection as a Leader

Leadership isn't a static state; it's a dynamic journey shaped by both external achievements and inner growth. The best leaders aren't just effective decision-makers or visionaries; they are intentional learners—curious, reflective, and open to development. They see leadership not as a destination but as an ongoing process of becoming.

At the core of sustained leadership growth is reflection—the intentional act of pausing to assess one's decisions, emotions, behaviours, and outcomes. In a world that rewards speed, reflection offers space for insight. In a culture that values action, it ensures that such action is rooted in wisdom.

Why Reflection Matters

It Transforms Experience into Insight

Experience alone does not foster growth. Reflection converts experience into understanding. It helps leaders identify patterns, test assumptions, and extract lessons that can be applied in the future.

It Increases Self-Awareness

Leaders who frequently reflect become more aware of their strengths, blind spots, emotional triggers, and values. This awareness enhances emotional regulation, improves interpersonal effectiveness, and fosters authenticity.

It Enhances Decision Quality

By examining past decisions—what went well, what didn't, and why—leaders develop sharper judgement and foresight.

It Builds Resilience

Reflection provides emotional processing. It helps leaders integrate failure, absorb feedback, and find meaning in adversity.

What Reflection Looks Like in Practice

Reflective leadership doesn't involve overthinking or rumination. It consists of asking intentional questions such as:
- What did I learn today?
- What emotions came up for me this week?
- Where did I lead well, and where did I hold back?
- What impact did I have on others?
- What patterns am I noticing in my responses?

These questions transform everyday leadership moments into opportunities for self-discovery and improvement.

Developing a Growth Mindset as a Leader

A reflective leader also embraces a growth mindset: the belief that leadership ability is developed, not fixed. This mindset:
- welcomes feedback, even when it's hard to hear
- sees mistakes as part of the process, not proof of inadequacy
- views challenge as opportunity, not threat.

When paired with regular reflection, a growth mindset creates a compounding effect. Learning accelerates, emotional maturity deepens, and leadership impact expands.

Obstacles to Reflection

Despite its benefits, many leaders struggle to reflect consistently. Common obstacles include:

Busyness
Packed schedules and urgent demands make it easy to skip reflection. But without it, leaders operate reactively instead of intentionally.

Fear of Vulnerability
Reflection requires honesty. Leaders may avoid looking inward to protect their ego or prevent discomfort.

Lack of Structure
Without a consistent process, such as journalling or regular coaching, reflection often remains vague or occasional.

Leaders need to establish a protected space and structured methods that make reflection a regular practice rather than an afterthought.

Integrating Reflection into Leadership Rhythm

Daily or Weekly Reviews
End each day or week with a brief self-inquiry:
- What was the most meaningful moment?
- Where did I lead well?
- What do I want to do differently next time?

Reflective Walks or Solitude
Taking unplugged walks or spending time alone away from screens can foster the mental clarity needed for reflection.

Post-Project or Decision Debriefs

After significant events, take time to reflect individually and as a team:
- What worked?
- What was challenging?
- What did we learn?

Debriefs foster shared learning and personal insight.

Leadership Journalling

Writing adds depth. It slows your thinking and reveals subconscious patterns. A leadership journal serves as a mirror for growth.

The Link Between Reflection and Strategic Thinking

Reflection sharpens strategy. When leaders reflect on the reasons behind their actions, not just the outcomes, they:
- see more clearly into the future
- anticipate unintended consequences
- adjust the course before problems escalate.

Strategic foresight is often rooted in hindsight. Reflection closes the loop between vision and reality.

Emotional Reflection: A Core Element of Growth

It's not just actions that deserve reflection; it's emotions. Emotionally reflective leaders ask:
- What did I feel in that moment and why?
- How did I manage my emotions?
- How did my emotional state affect others?

This fosters emotional agility, the ability to recognise, understand, and manage emotions in constructive ways.

Creating a Culture of Reflection in Your Team

Leaders who model reflection also invite it in others. You can:
- ask team members to share lessons learned
- build "pause moments" into project cycles
- celebrate growth, not just results
- make feedback safe and normalised.

A reflective culture promotes learning, humility, and psychological safety. It shifts the team from execution mode to growth mode.

The Long-Term Payoff: Adaptive, Wise Leadership

Leaders who build a life of reflection tend to:
- adapt more quickly in complex environments
- lead with deeper self-awareness and empathy
- recover faster from failure
- inspire trust through authenticity and reliability.

They don't merely grow in title; they grow in wisdom. In a world that urgently needs wise leadership, that might be the most valuable growth of all.

Reflection Is a Leadership Discipline

Reflection is not a retreat from leadership; rather, it is a practice that strengthens it. It transforms action into insight, pressure into presence, and experience into growth.

Leaders who take a moment to reflect don't slow down; they sharpen their focus. They see further and lead more profoundly.

If you want to grow as a leader, don't just do more; do it better. Think more. Feel more. Reflect more. The leader you're becoming is shaped by the awareness you bring to every choice, every conversation, and every challenge.

Journalling, Coaching, and Feedback Loops

Leadership is a high-stakes, emotionally complex, and constantly evolving journey. To remain grounded and practical, leaders need not only intelligence and drive but also tools for self-reflection, accountability, and feedback. Three of the most effective tools for sustained growth are journalling, coaching, and feedback loops.

These tools help leaders understand not only what they do but also why they do it and how they can improve. Collectively, they create a feedback-rich ecosystem that promotes self-awareness, learning agility, and behavioural transformation.

Leadership Journalling: A Mirror for the Mind

Journalling is more than just keeping a diary. It is a deliberate practice of slowing down, thinking deeply, and processing experiences. For leaders, journalling offers a private space to:
- make sense of complex events
- clarify goals, thoughts, and decisions
- track emotional states and triggers
- reflect on personal growth.

Benefits of Journalling for Leaders
- *Enhanced self-awareness*: Reflecting on daily experiences reveals patterns in thinking, behaviour, and emotions.
- *Stress reduction*: Journalling can lessen emotional intensity by externalising pressure and assisting leaders in processing stress constructively.
- *Better decision-making*: By reflecting on lessons learned from past challenges, leaders can pinpoint what was effective, what wasn't, and the reasons behind those outcomes.
- *Stronger emotional intelligence*: Identifying emotions in writing enhances emotional vocabulary and regulation.

Practical Approaches to Leadership Journalling
- *Daily reflections*: What did I learn today? What went well? What were my challenges?
- *Decision logs*: What was the decision? What options did I consider? What influenced my choice?
- *Emotional check-ins*: How am I feeling? Why? What's behind that emotion?
- *Weekly lessons*: What themes or patterns emerged this week?

Even ten minutes a day can yield significant insights over time. The key is consistency, not perfection.

Executive Coaching: Guided Self-Discovery

Coaching offers a structured and supportive environment for leaders to explore their goals, challenges, and areas for growth and improvement. A coach is neither a therapist nor a

consultant; they serve as a thinking partner to assist leaders in their personal and professional development, helping them:
- clarify what they want
- examine how they think and act
- build new mental models and habits
- stay accountable for change.

Why Coaching Works

It's Personalised
Coaching is tailored to the leader's context, values, and areas for growth.

It Promotes Reflection During Action
Sessions frequently involve real-time reflection on recent situations or decisions.

It Provides a Safe Space
Coaches offer confidentiality, non-judgement, and constructive challenge.

It Supports Behavioural Change
Coaching assists leaders in transforming awareness into action and reflection into results.

Leaders benefit most when they come to coaching open, committed, and willing to be honest with themselves.

Topics Commonly Explored in Coaching
- Strategic clarity and decision-making
- Emotional regulation and resilience
- Communication and influence
- Navigating conflict or change
- Leadership identity and impostor syndrome
- Team dynamics and culture shaping

When paired with journalling, coaching becomes even more effective. Journals offer data, while coaching helps derive meaning from it.

Feedback Loops: The Engine of Growth

Feedback serves as the bridge between intention and impact. Leaders might believe they're being clear, inspiring, or empathetic, but only feedback can show how others perceive them.

The Power of Feedback Loops

A feedback loop is more than receiving feedback once. It's a continuous cycle.

- *Input*: Seek and receive feedback.
- *Reflection*: Process and analyse what you hear.
- *Adaptation*: Adjust behaviours and strategies accordingly.
- *Follow-up*: Check back to see if the impact has improved.

Leaders who master this loop become agile learners.

Why Many Leaders Avoid Feedback

- Fear of criticism
- Worry about losing authority
- Discomfort with vulnerability
- Past experiences with poorly delivered feedback

Yet without feedback, growth stalls. Blind spots continue. Assumptions remain untested.

Creating a Healthy Feedback Culture

Start by modelling it yourself.

- Ask regularly: "What's one thing I could do better?"
- Respond with gratitude, not defensiveness.
- Act visibly on feedback when possible.
- Create rituals for team feedback (after projects, quarterly check-ins, etc.).

Feedback doesn't always need to be formal. The more embedded it is in daily leadership, the more effective it becomes.

Integrating the Three Tools

These tools are strongest when used together.

Tool	Function	Result
Journalling	Internal insight and pattern recognition	Self-awareness and emotional clarity
Coaching	Guided reflection and accountability	Strategic growth and behaviour change
Feedback loops	External validation and course correction	Alignment and influence improvement

Maintaining a journalling habit can help prepare for coaching sessions. Coaching can help leaders take action on the feedback they receive. Feedback can inspire fresh journal reflections. Together, they promote continuous growth.

Building a Routine for Reflective Practice

A simple rhythm to embed these tools:

- **Daily**: 5–10 minutes of journalling at the end of the day.
- **Weekly**: Review journal entries; reflect on highs/lows; prepare notes for coaching.

- **Monthly**: Receive structured feedback from a peer, team member, or mentor.
- **Quarterly**: Engage in a formal coaching session or self-review based on key leadership goals.

The key is consistency and integration. Make growth a discipline, not a side project.

When the Tools Lead to Transformation

Leaders who engage in structured reflection often:
- develop stronger emotional regulation
- catch limiting beliefs and reframe them
- lead with more empathy and clarity
- create stronger team relationships and outcomes
- feel more fulfilled and less isolated in their role.

Their leadership matures, not just in performance but in presence. They lead with intention, not reaction. With insight, not ego.

Growth Is Intentional

Journalling, coaching, and feedback loops are not exclusive to struggling leaders; they are essential tools for wise leaders. Leaders who know that reflection is not a pause from progress but the source of it, leaders who understand that the best way to grow others is by first developing themselves.

Leadership is not just about guiding others; it is also about inspiring them to achieve their goals. It's about knowing yourself. And there is no substitute for the kind of structured, intentional self-inquiry that these tools provide.

So write. Reflect. Seek insight. Embrace feedback. Allow the loop of learning to become the rhythm of your leadership.

Emotional Growth as a Leadership Edge

Leadership is more than strategy, execution, and decision-making. At its core, it is the management of human energy, yours and others'. That's why one of the most underappreciated yet powerful dimensions of leadership is emotional growth. In an era defined by complexity, disruption, and relational tension, emotional growth is no longer a "nice-to-have"; it is a competitive edge.

Emotionally mature leaders foster deeper trust, inspire greater commitment, recover more quickly from setbacks, and lead more sustainable teams. They understand themselves and others with nuance and sensitivity. They turn emotional intelligence into practical influence. They grow not just in title but in depth.

What Is Emotional Growth?

Emotional growth is the process of developing emotional insight, resilience, and maturity. It involves:

- becoming aware of your emotional triggers and patterns

- increasing your capacity to manage and express emotions constructively
- developing empathy for others' emotional experiences
- integrating emotional insight into how you lead, relate, and decide.

It's not about being emotional. It's about being emotionally agile, able to recognise, regulate, and respond to emotion wisely.

Why Emotional Growth Matters Now More Than Ever

The workplace has changed. So has the emotional landscape leaders must navigate including:
- rising stress, burnout, and mental health challenges
- generational shifts in emotional expectations and values
- remote and hybrid work, creating emotional distance
- rapid change and uncertainty, increasing collective anxiety.

In this environment, leaders who overlook emotional dynamics lose connection. Leaders who foster emotional growth develop relational authority, a form of leadership that earns trust through authenticity, empathy, and steadiness.

The Link Between Emotional Growth and Leadership Impact

Leaders who develop emotionally unlock greater performance in themselves and their teams.

Emotional Self-Awareness Leads to Improved Decision-Making

When leaders are aware of the emotions influencing their decisions, they become less reactive and more reflective. They take a moment before responding and opt for intention over impulse.

Emotional Regulation Leads to a Consistent Presence

Emotionally mature leaders don't spike with mood swings or crash under pressure. They remain steady, grounded, and composed, especially when it matters most.

Empathy Leads to a More Profound Influence

Empathy builds trust. It allows leaders to connect with what their people need, not just procedurally but emotionally. This makes motivation more human and communication more effective.

Emotional Resilience Leads to Sustainable Leadership

Emotional growth enables leaders to recover from failure, handle criticism effectively, and maintain optimism in the face of uncertainty. This stamina is what sustains leadership in the face of complexity.

Emotional Growth in Action: Observable Traits

Emotionally growing leaders tend to:
- ask reflective questions after difficult situations
- take ownership of their emotional impact
- apologise when they react poorly and learn from it
- seek feedback about their relational blind spots
- read the emotional climate of a room before speaking
- show compassion without rescuing or enabling.

These are not personality traits. They are practised behaviours that emerge through conscious development.

Developing Emotional Growth as a Discipline

Like any growth area, emotional development requires deliberate effort. Here's how leaders can cultivate it.

Regular Self-Inquiry

Ask:
- What am I feeling and why?
- What part of me was activated in that meeting?
- Did my emotions serve or sabotage my leadership?

Reflection increases emotional literacy.

Learning From Triggers

Instead of avoiding what frustrates you, explore it:
- What is this reaction showing me about my values, insecurities, or past experiences?
- How can I respond from a place of alignment rather than reactivity?

Your emotional triggers are teachers in disguise.

Emotional Journalling

Writing about emotions sharpens awareness and supports regulation. Keep a log of emotional highs and lows, noting patterns and insights.

Emotional Role Models

Observe leaders who demonstrate emotional strength, warmth, or grace. Ask:
- What do they do in moments of pressure?
- How do they express empathy or accountability?
- What emotional habits can I adopt or refine?

Leadership is as much caught as it is taught.

Integrating Emotional Growth into Your Leadership Style

Emotional growth isn't a separate domain; it should infuse how you:

- *Set vision*: Speak with emotional resonance, not just facts.
- *Hold performance conversations*: Balance honesty with care.
- *Navigate conflict*: Acknowledge emotions while maintaining boundaries.
- *Lead change*: Honour grief and uncertainty, not just plans and timelines.

It is what transforms "management" into human leadership.

How Emotional Growth Becomes a Cultural Multiplier

Your emotional growth shapes the emotional tone of your team and organisation. Leaders who lead from a place of maturity create:

- safer environments for candour and risk-taking
- greater emotional resilience across teams
- a culture where feedback, empathy, and emotional honesty are normal.

When a leader is emotionally grounded, people perform better, not because they're pushed but because they feel seen, supported, and inspired.

Obstacles to Emotional Growth in Leadership

Emotional development can be uncomfortable. Leaders may resist it because of:

- *Fear of vulnerability*: Believing emotion makes them look weak.
- *Pace of execution*: Feeling too busy to pause and reflect.
- *Cultural norms*: Operating in environments where emotions are avoided or dismissed.
- *Past wounds*: Carrying emotional trauma that remains unexamined.

But these challenges are not roadblocks; they are invitations. To face discomfort is to grow. To avoid it is to stay stuck.

Measuring Progress in Emotional Growth

It's not always easy to track emotional development, but signs include:

- reacting less and responding more
- feeling calm in situations that once triggered anxiety
- receiving feedback about being more present or grounded
- finding language to name what you're feeling, instead of suppressing it
- noticing others feel safer or more connected in your presence.

The internal shift is fundamental, and the external impact is visible.

Emotional Growth Is Your Leadership Advantage

In the future of leadership, the most successful leaders won't just be those with technical expertise or positional power. They will be the ones who can navigate the emotional landscape of themselves and others with courage, humility, and wisdom.

Emotional growth enables you to remain human while leading others. It keeps your leadership anchored in empathy, aligned with purpose, and responsive to the reality of others.

It's not a soft skill; it's a core advantage. And as you continue to grow emotionally, you don't just become a better leader. You become a more whole and impactful person, the kind of leader people remember, trust, and choose to follow.

The Integrated Leader: Wholeness at the Heart of Leadership

Leadership today demands more than knowledge or charisma; it requires integration and synthesis of knowledge and charisma. An integrated leader is someone who brings their whole self to the role, encompassing intellect and intuition, logic and emotion, as well as strength and vulnerability. Competing identities or roles do not fragment them. Instead, they lead from a place of internal coherence and alignment.

In a world of complexity, volatility, and rapid change, integration becomes a leader's most powerful stabiliser. It brings clarity amidst chaos, authenticity amidst performance pressure, and depth amidst surface-level noise. The integrated leader is grounded, self-aware, and able to lead with consistency, empathy, and ethical clarity.

What Does It Mean to Be an Integrated Leader?

Integration is the process of bringing together different parts of the self, including rational, emotional, ethical, and relational aspects, into a cohesive whole. An integrated leader:

- aligns values, actions, and words

- balances intellect with emotional intelligence
- embodies authenticity, not just image
- makes decisions that serve both the purpose and the people
- brings personal growth and professional responsibility into harmony.

This is not perfection. It is congruence. Integrated leaders lead from a place of wholeness.

Why Integration Matters in Leadership

Consistency Builds Trust

People trust leaders who are consistent in their private and public behaviour. Integrated leaders are not performing; they are present.

Alignment Drives Impact

When a leader's vision, decisions, and behaviours align, energy flows more freely. Fragmentation leads to confusion; integration leads to clarity and execution.

Resilience Comes from Inner Unity

In turbulent times, integrated leaders don't collapse under pressure. They draw on the depth of self-knowledge, inner alignment, and a secure identity.

Ethical Leadership Requires Integration

Ethical lapses often come from compartmentalisation, separating values from behaviour. Integration ensures decisions are anchored in both character and context.

The Fragmented Leader: A Cautionary Contrast

By contrast, fragmented leaders:

- project a professional image while hiding inner struggle
- prioritise intellect but dismiss emotional cues
- compromise values under pressure
- react from ego rather than grounded awareness.

Others feel this dissonance. It creates confusion, distrust, and inconsistency in leadership culture.

Key Dimensions of Integrated Leadership

Self-Awareness

Integrated leaders know who they are. They have done the inner work to understand their values, emotional patterns, and leadership purpose. They lead from identity, not insecurity.

Emotional Intelligence

They recognise and manage their emotions while understanding those of others. They don't suppress emotion; they integrate it into how they lead.

Strategic Thinking

They balance vision with analysis. They see the big picture without losing sight of relational or emotional dynamics.

Integrity

They do what's right, even when it's hard. Their actions are a reflection of their values, not their circumstances.

Relational Depth

They foster genuine connections. Their leadership isn't transactional; it's transformational, rooted in empathy and human dignity.

The Path to Becoming an Integrated Leader

Integration isn't just a personality trait; it's a journey and a daily commitment to self-awareness, reflection, and alignment.

Step 1: Identify the Gaps

Where do you feel most divided as a leader?
- Do you hide parts of yourself to maintain control or image?
- Do your values and behaviours align?
- Do you show up differently in different settings?

Awareness is the first step towards integration.

Step 2: Do the Inner Work

This includes:
- regular reflection or journaling
- seeking feedback on your experience
- exploring emotional triggers or fears
- clarifying your leadership "why".

Leadership growth starts with personal development.

Step 3: Lead From the Inside Out

Make choices that embody your values, not merely external pressures. Communicate and behave in ways that resonate with your identity. Lead with purpose, not just performance.

The Organisational Impact of Integrated Leadership

Integrated leaders foster integrated cultures. They exemplify what it means to:
- be real, not perfect
- balance data with empathy
- honour both results and relationships
- lead with courage and humility.

This fosters psychological safety, trust, and shared ownership throughout the organisation.

Myths That Undermine Integration

"Vulnerability is weakness."
Truth: Vulnerability is where trust and innovation begin.

"Emotions don't belong at work."
Truth: Unacknowledged emotions continue to influence the workplace, often in a destructive manner.

"Leaders should always have the answers."
Truth: Integrated leaders ask better questions and cultivate collective wisdom.

"Professionalism means being detached."
Truth: True professionalism is about being fully present with people and upholding integrity in all actions.

Practices That Support Integrated Leadership

- Mindfulness or grounding routines to stay present
- Values-based decision frameworks
- Regular coaching or mentoring for an external perspective
- Team debriefs that include emotional and cultural reflection
- Leadership journalling to connect inner and outer worlds

These practices nurture integration as a way of being, rather than merely a technique.

Leading With Wholeness

The integrated leader may not be perfect, but they are whole. They have undertaken the hard work of self-reflection, emotional growth, and aligning their values. They lead with coherence, authenticity, and clarity of purpose.

By doing this, they not only achieve outcomes but also reshape the culture surrounding them.

In an age that craves authentic, discerning, and well-founded leadership, integration isn't just a soft skill; it's a strategic essential.

Leading With Both Head and Heart

Leadership has long been associated with traits such as decisiveness, logic, and rationality, which are often seen as the domain of the head. However, today's most effective leaders recognise that intellect alone is no longer enough. To lead in a world of rapid change, emotional complexity, and human-centred expectations, leaders must also draw on the wisdom of the heart.

Leading with both head and heart means combining analytical thinking with emotional intelligence, strategic foresight with human empathy, and operational precision with moral courage. This integrated leadership style doesn't dilute results; it deepens them. It not only elevates what is achieved but also how it is achieved, and who is brought along the way.

What It Means to Lead with the Head

The head represents cognitive and strategic leadership skills and attributes such as:
- analytical thinking
- decision-making under pressure

- systematic planning
- problem-solving
- data-driven evaluation
- clarity of direction.

This kind of leadership is vital for managing complexity, aligning teams with their objectives, and navigating uncertainty. It enables leaders to stay focused, ask the right questions, and make effective and timely decisions.

However, concentrating solely on the head can become overly clinical. This approach may result in disconnection, rigidity, or blind spots when emotional dynamics or people-centred factors are ignored.

What It Means to Lead with the Heart

The heart represents the emotional and relational side of leadership. It includes:
- empathy
- compassion
- authenticity
- emotional intuition
- active listening
- connection and care.

Leading with heart means showing up as fully human. It involves recognising the emotional climate of your team, responding to people's needs, and nurturing a culture of psychological safety. Heart-led leadership strengthens trust, loyalty, and resilience.

However, a heart without a head runs the risk of sentimentality, a lack of direction, and emotional exhaustion. The magic lies in integration.

Why Leading with Both Is Essential

The combination of head and heart allows leaders to:
- make wise and thoughtful decisions
- develop strategies that inspire people to act
- enhance performance while maintaining wellbeing
- manage metrics while retaining meaning
- cultivate cultures that are focused on results and rich in relationships.

In short, leadership that balances head and heart empowers organisations to be high-performing and human.

The Neuroscience of Head and Heart

Even neuroscience supports the value of integration. The brain's prefrontal cortex oversees rational thinking and decision-making, while the limbic system manages emotion and social connection. Exceptional leadership engages both.

Emotional intelligence is not separate from cognition; it enhances it. Leaders with high emotional intelligence:
- read signals more accurately
- regulate their emotional state for better judgement
- build trust that increases team effectiveness.

Thinking and feeling aren't rivals; they are partners in achieving leadership success.

Examples of Head-and-Heart Leadership in Action

- A CEO who makes a difficult restructuring decision (head) yet communicates it with transparency and empathy for those affected (heart).
- A team leader who monitors KPIs and deadlines (head) while assessing team morale and burnout (heart).

- A public leader who develops data-driven policies (head) while authentically considering the lived experiences of citizens (heart).
- A manager who sets high expectations (head) but supports employees through challenges and development (heart).

This is not about balancing opposites; it's about blending disciplines into a cohesive leadership presence.

Developing the Head and the Heart as a Leader

Strengthening the Head
- Read broadly across economics, strategy, history, and systems thinking.
- Practise using structured decision-making models.
- Seek mentors who challenge your reasoning and viewpoint.
- Use after-action reviews to learn from outcomes.

Strengthening the Heart
- Develop self-awareness via reflection and journalling.
- Practice empathy by asking open-ended questions and listening attentively.
- Understand trauma-informed leadership and psychological safety.
- Seek coaching to uncover emotional blind spots.

Leaders develop more effectively when they deliberately nurture both domains and allow them to influence each other.

Challenges in Leading with Both

Some leaders lean heavily on one domain and neglect the other. Common patterns include:

- *Overthinking without connection*: Strategy seems cold or detached from people.
- *Feeling deeply without clarity*: Compassion is powerful but guidance is unclear.
- *Emotional suppression*: The act of suppressing emotions to maintain control which ultimately erodes trust.
- *Over-identifying with emotions*: This can lead to losing objectivity or overcompensating for approval.

These extremes can be balanced by asking:
- "Is my heart guiding this without losing my head?"
- "Is my head leading this without disconnecting from people?"

Head and Heart in Crisis Leadership

During crises, head and heart leadership become critical.
- The head ensures decisions are timely, informed, and strategic.
- The heart ensures communication is human, clear, and compassionate.

Leaders who do both:
- acknowledge fear without amplifying it
- maintain hope while being honest
- act quickly without being careless
- empower others even under duress.

People don't just remember what leaders did in a crisis; they remember how it felt to be led by them.

The Legacy of Head-and-Heart Leaders

The most impactful leaders throughout history, such as Nelson Mandela, Jacinda Ardern, and Fred Rogers, have shown the ability to lead with intellectual strength and moral compassion. They held brutal truths with grace, guided people through fear with calmness, and inspired transformation with both courage and care.

Their legacies remind us that how we lead is just as important as what we achieve.

Integration Is the Future of Leadership

Leading with both head and heart means being a whole person. It involves making decisions with clarity and conscience, pursuing goals while remembering people, and wielding power to foster shared progress, rather than mere personal ambition.

In today's world, technical competence is expected, while emotional competence is what sets leaders apart.

So the question is no longer, "Should I lead with head or heart?"

The question is, "How do I lead with both, consistently and courageously?"

That's the work. That's the edge. That's the future.

Embodying Emotional Integrity in Everyday Leadership

Leadership isn't merely about strategy or execution; it's fundamentally about presence. At the core of authentic presence lies emotional integrity: the ability to acknowledge, own, and express your emotions honestly and responsibly, in alignment with your values and the needs of those you lead.

Emotional integrity is the cornerstone of trust. It forges the connection between a leader's inner world and outward behaviour. It's what makes a leader credible, not because they're always right but because they're honest, grounded, and transparent.

In a world where people are increasingly sensitive to inauthenticity, emotional integrity is not merely a moral imperative; it's a strategic advantage.

What Is Emotional Integrity?

Emotional integrity is the ongoing practice of being emotionally honest with yourself and others. It signifies:

- acknowledging your feelings without suppressing or becoming overly attached to them
- expressing your emotions in constructive ways that align with your values

- taking responsibility for your emotional influence
- choosing honesty over harmony when the truth is at stake.

It's not about being emotional; it's about being emotionally congruent, where your inner state, your communication, and your behaviour align.

Why Emotional Integrity Matters

It Builds Trust
People trust authentic leaders. Emotional integrity encourages transparency and consistency. Team members understand their position and what to expect.

It Promotes Psychological Safety
When a leader demonstrates emotional openness, it fosters a safe environment in which others can express their thoughts, concerns, and ideas without fear of ridicule or retribution.

It Strengthens Decision-Making
When leaders ignore or distort their emotions, their decisions are likely to be tainted by bias. Emotional integrity ensures that decisions take into account both rational analysis and emotional impact.

It Enhances Relational Depth
Teams become more cohesive and committed when led by someone who incorporates emotional authenticity into their leadership style.

What Emotional Integrity Looks Like in Practice
- Saying, "I'm frustrated by what happened, but I want to understand before I react."

- Admitting, "I'm uncertain right now, and I'll be honest about what I don't know."
- Letting your team know, "That decision was tough. I've been reflecting on its impact."
- Apologising for a misstep without deflecting or justifying.
- Communicating emotions with clarity instead of passive aggression or silence.

These behaviours indicate that emotions are not concealed or weaponised; they are embraced and integrated.

The Cost of Lacking Emotional Integrity

Leaders who lack emotional integrity may:

- suppress their emotions until they erupt as anger or withdrawal
- use manipulation or ambiguity to avoid brutal truths
- perform leadership instead of embodying it
- create confusion, tension, or distrust among their teams.

Even highly competent leaders lose influence when emotional incongruence arises. People perceive the disconnect between what's said and what's truly felt.

Practising Emotional Integrity in Daily Leadership

Name Your Emotions

If you can't name what you feel, you can't work with it. Cultivate emotional granularity and the ability to discern between different emotions, such as frustration, disappointment, shame, and fear.

Ask:
- What am I feeling?
- Where is it coming from?
- What value is being challenged?

Reflect Before You React

Emotional integrity does not equate to raw expression; instead, it refers to regulated expression. Before speaking or acting:
- breathe
- reflect on what matters
- ask yourself, "What does integrity look like here?"

Speak the Truth with Compassion

When something hard needs to be said, say it, but in a way that honours both the truth and the dignity of the other person.

You can be honest and kind. Direct and caring. Emotionally honest and emotionally mature.

Own Your Impact

If your emotional state negatively affects others, take responsibility for it. Say:
- I realise I came across as harsh; I was overwhelmed, but that's no excuse.
- My tone wasn't helpful in that meeting. I'll approach it differently next time.

Accountability restores trust faster than perfection.

Stay Aligned Under Pressure

Pressure often tempts leaders to abandon their emotional integrity and to:
- conceal fear with arrogance
- manage grief with detachment

- replace honesty with control.

But pressure is precisely when emotional integrity matters most. It's when people look for signs of steadiness and authenticity.

Common Challenges to Emotional Integrity

Fear of Vulnerability

Some leaders are afraid that being emotionally honest will make them appear weak. However, it increases their credibility and trustworthiness.

Culture of Suppression

In some organisations, emotions are viewed as unprofessional. However, ignoring emotions results in hidden dysfunction.

Ego and Control

Leaders might hide their genuine feelings to maintain control or protect their ego. However, this results in emotional distance and undermines team connection.

Overcoming these challenges requires courage and consciousness.

Creating a Culture of Emotional Integrity

When a leader demonstrates emotional integrity, others tend to follow suit. You can:

- normalise discussions about emotional experiences during debriefs
- recognise not only performance but also emotional labour and honesty
- establish clear expectations for respectful emotional expression

- provide coaching and feedback on emotional impact.

Emotional integrity serves as a cultural anchor, something that people feel, trust, and replicate.

Emotional Integrity vs. Emotional Perfectionism

Emotional integrity doesn't mean you always get it right; it means:
- you reflect and learn when you don't
- you're honest when things are unclear
- you're present even when it's uncomfortable
- you aim to be emotionally congruent, rather than emotionally flawless.

The goal isn't to suppress your emotions or be endlessly open; it's about embodying honesty with wisdom.

Lead From Within

To embody emotional integrity means leading from the inside out. It signifies that your leadership is grounded not only in goals or vision but also in the honest, courageous, and consistent practice of emotional self-awareness.

It means you show up not as a persona but as a complete person. And in doing so, you create space for others to do the same.

Every email, every meeting, every moment of pressure presents an opportunity to choose integrity. To align who you are with how you lead. To earn trust not through charm or certainty but through truth, vulnerability, and consistency.

That's the kind of leadership the world needs. That's the kind of leadership that endures.

Personal Reflection: Leadership That Lasts

I used to believe that resilience meant pushing through, regardless of the circumstances. That being a strong leader was about carrying the weight, keeping going, and never showing cracks. And for a while, that belief served me. It got me through high-stakes decisions, challenging transitions, and long nights.

However, it took its toll on me, and over time, I began to notice that something was amiss. I was getting results, but I was emotionally worn out. I was depleted, snappier with people I cared about, and disconnected from the meaning behind the work. I thought I just needed a break. What I needed was a reckoning.

Burnout isn't always obvious. Sometimes, it sneaks in through good intentions or the desire to serve, the sense of duty, the pressure to be reliable. But no one leads well when they're running on empty. And I was empty.

That period in my life taught me one of the most challenging and vital lessons in my leadership journey: you can't sustainably lead others if you neglect yourself in the process.

I started doing something unfamiliar for me, and I slowed down. I began saying no. I reflected, becoming curious about my emotional patterns. I sought feedback, not just about what I was doing but about how I was being. I allowed myself to feel the fatigue I had long ignored and permitted myself to recover.

In that space, I found something I hadn't felt in a long time: wholeness and peace. Not perfection. Not performance. Just an honest return to myself. And from that place, I came back stronger, not just in energy but also in clarity and conviction.

Maintaining the emotional resilience of leadership isn't about working through alone. It's about recognising when to push on and when to take a breather. When to speak up and when to listen inward. When to give and when to replenish.

The most powerful leaders I know aren't the ones who've never burned out. They're the ones who've come back, with more wisdom, more empathy, and more wholeness than before.

That's the sort of leader I aim to be. I hope you choose to be the same.

Conclusion: The Journey Home to Self, Team, and Purpose

Leadership isn't just a title, a salary band, or a seat at the table; it's a mindset. It's a way of being, grounded not only in strategic foresight and operational excellence but also in emotional integrity, relational courage, and the willingness to stand firm amid uncertainty. This book has examined the emotional dimensions of leadership, not as peripheral traits to be managed but as core capacities to cultivate. What emerges isn't a soft or indulgent portrait of leadership; instead, it presents one of radical responsibility, where leading with heart is both the most human and the most strategic path forward.

At the heart of this journey lies the emotional compass, a metaphor for the internal guidance system that great leaders craft and refine over time. Like any compass, it requires calibration. The storms of stress, ego, or fear can disrupt it. However, when steady, it directs us towards the authentic centre of who we are, what we value, and how we serve.

Let's reflect on what it genuinely means to lead through this lens.

The Inner Landscape

Leading others starts with leading ourselves. This truth, echoed in various forms throughout leadership literature, often becomes a cliché. However, in emotionally intelligent leadership, it transforms into a call for inner mastery. Self-awareness, emotional regulation, vulnerability, and self-compassion are not luxuries; they're prerequisites for sustained performance and personal integrity.

You can't cultivate psychological safety in others if you're living in fear. You can't ask for trust without offering truth. You can't inspire if your emotional energy is depleted. And you can't expect a team to follow you into uncertainty if you haven't yet made peace with your own.

Leaders must become comfortable navigating the terrain of their own emotions: anger, joy, sadness, fear, shame, and hope. These are not distractions from logic or strategy; they are the raw signals of meaning, values, and boundaries. Ignoring them is akin to leading in a fog. Harnessing them enables one to lead with clarity and conviction.

The Relational Space

Teams function as emotional systems. Culture isn't just a policy; it's a feeling. The mood in a workplace directly reflects the emotional climate established by its leaders. Tone, trust, empathy, presence—these are the levers of high-performance cultures, and all of them are rooted in emotion.

Leadership is not solely about individual effectiveness; it also involves emotional transmission. How you present yourself emotionally influences the performance of others. If you lead with defensiveness, you create an atmosphere of avoidance. If you lead with compassion and accountability, you encourage courage. If you lead with curiosity, you facilitate innovation. If you lead with apathy, you receive silence.

Trust is built not through grand gestures but through the daily consistency of your emotional presence. Feedback conversations, crisis meetings, team celebrations, and performance reviews each provide a chance to lead emotionally, either fostering connection or eroding it.

The leader who learns to navigate conflict with empathy, offers feedback without shame, and models accountability without ego becomes not merely a manager of work but a builder of people.

The Organisational Horizon

In times of volatility, complexity, and change, emotional leadership transforms into strategic leadership. Traditional metrics, KPIs, dashboards, and market analysis remain significant, but they are no longer sufficient to meet the evolving needs of businesses. Emotional signals now serve as early indicators of risk and opportunity.

An unengaged workforce is a significant warning sign, well before attrition figures appear. A culture of silence often leads to ethical failures. An anxious team typically indicates a misalignment with its values or a lack of clarity. The emotionally aware leader pays attention to these signals and responds before they escalate.

This isn't soft; it's smart. Emotionally intelligent leadership enhances decision-making, strengthens ethical behaviour, improves employee retention, and boosts adaptability. In short, it's a competitive advantage.

Emotionally grounded leadership is what builds lasting legacies. As economies evolve and technologies change, the most sustainable resource is human connection. Leaders who understand the emotional ecosystem of their organisations will thrive in the future, not despite their humanity but because of it.

The Courage to Feel

Emotional leadership is often uncomfortable. It asks us to slow down, to listen, and to feel. It demands that we confront our own biases, pain, and projections. It requires the courage to say, "I don't know" or "I got it wrong." It invites humility instead of bravado and depth rather than mere performance.

However, the payoff is significant.

The emotionally mature leader isn't perfect; they're genuine. They can navigate complexity, create space for multiple truths, and act based on their principles. They don't hide behind protocol when compassion is necessary. They won't outsource accountability. They choose the long road because they understand that shortcuts erode trust.

These leaders are the ones people choose to follow, not out of obligation but out of desire. These are the leaders who transform lives, not just balance sheets.

The Call to Integration

The emotional compass isn't about swinging to the opposite extreme, where you lead only with feelings and abandon rigour. It's about integration. The head and the heart. Strategy and empathy. Strength and softness.

Integrated leaders do not compartmentalise their humanity; they embody it. They do not see emotion as a liability but as data. They do not chase perfection; they pursue presence. And in doing so, they inspire teams to show up more fully, contribute more boldly, and believe more deeply in the mission.

Your role as a leader isn't to control every variable; it's to create conditions that enable people to thrive, and that includes you.

So, calibrate your emotional compass regularly. In times of pressure, revisit your values. In moments of doubt, reflect on your purpose. In seasons of growth, embrace humility. In times of joy, cultivate gratitude.

A Final Reflection

The journey of emotionally grounded leadership is a lifelong one. There is no final destination, only a deeper expression of what it means to be human while leading other humans.

But along the way, you will notice shifts:
- Conversations will deepen.
- Performance will improve.
- Trust will grow stronger.
- And your leadership will become not only practical but also meaningful.

People will remember how you made them feel, how you saw them, heard them, valued them, challenged them, and made them feel safe. They will mirror your presence, not your title. They will grow not just because of your vision but also due to your emotional integrity.

This is the power of emotional leadership. It doesn't shout. It resonates. It doesn't demand. It invites. It doesn't fracture. It integrates.

Let your leadership be guided not just by what you know but by who you are. Lead with your emotional compass steady, your purpose clear, and your heart open.

In the end, the most powerful leaders aren't just the ones who get things done; they're the ones who help others become more of who they truly are.

It all starts with you.

References

Brown, B. (2010, June). The Power of Vulnerability. Houston, Texas, United States: TEDxHouston. Retrieved from https://youtu.be/iCvmsMzlF7o?si=qA47aVyNwNj5qy3C

Brown, B. (2012). *Daring greatly: How the courage to be vulnerable transforms the way we live, love, parent and lead.* New York: Gotham Books.

Commission, A. P. (2021). *SES Performance Leadership Framework.* Retrieved from www.apsc.gov.au: chrome-extension://efaidnbmnnnibpcajpcglclefindmkaj/https://www.apsc.gov.au/sites/default/files/2023-08/SES%20performance%20leadership%20framework%20-%20Integrity%20and%20psychological%20safety%20for%20leaders.pdf

Edmondson, A. (2019, January 22). *Creating Psychological Safety in the Workplace.* Retrieved from Harvard Business Review: https://hbr.org/podcast/2019/01/creating-psychological-safety-in-the-workplace

Goleman, D. (1998). *Working with emotional intelligence.* New York: Bantam Books.

Goleman, D. (2020). *Emotional Intelligence: Why it can matter more than IQ.* New York: Bantam Books Inc.

Neff, D. K. (n.d.). *The Three Components of Self-Compassion.* Retrieved May 23, 2025, from selfcompassion.web.unc.edu: https://selfcompassion.web.unc.edu/what-is-self-compassion/the-three-components-of-self-compassion/

About the Author

Blake Repine spent more than 18 and a half years in various roles in the US Army before transitioning into the corporate world. He is a senior executive and non-executive director with more than 20 years' experience in providing strategic vision, leadership, and executive management. Blake has expertise in leadership and building strong, positive organisational cultures. He formulates strategies to drive improvement and innovation across a range of large and diverse organisations. Blake has facilitated growth within organisations by establishing targeted solutions and strategic plans to improve operational efficiency and leadership effectiveness.

As well as having attended multiple leadership courses in the Army, Blake also possesses a Bachelor of Science in Multidisciplinary Studies and a Master of Arts in Management and Leadership from Liberty University, along with an MBA from Norwich University and a Certificate of Completion in Disruptive Strategy from Harvard Business School. Blake is a certified professional with the Australian Human Resources Institute (AHRI), a member of the Institute of Public Accountants (IPA), and a member of the Australian Institute of Company Director's (AICD).

Blake lives in Australia with his family. In his spare time, Blake enjoys fishing, camping, scuba diving, rock climbing, and riding motorcycles. He is also an active volunteer in his community.

www.ingramcontent.com/pod-product-compliance
Lightning Source LLC
Chambersburg PA
CBHW031235290426
44109CB00012B/301